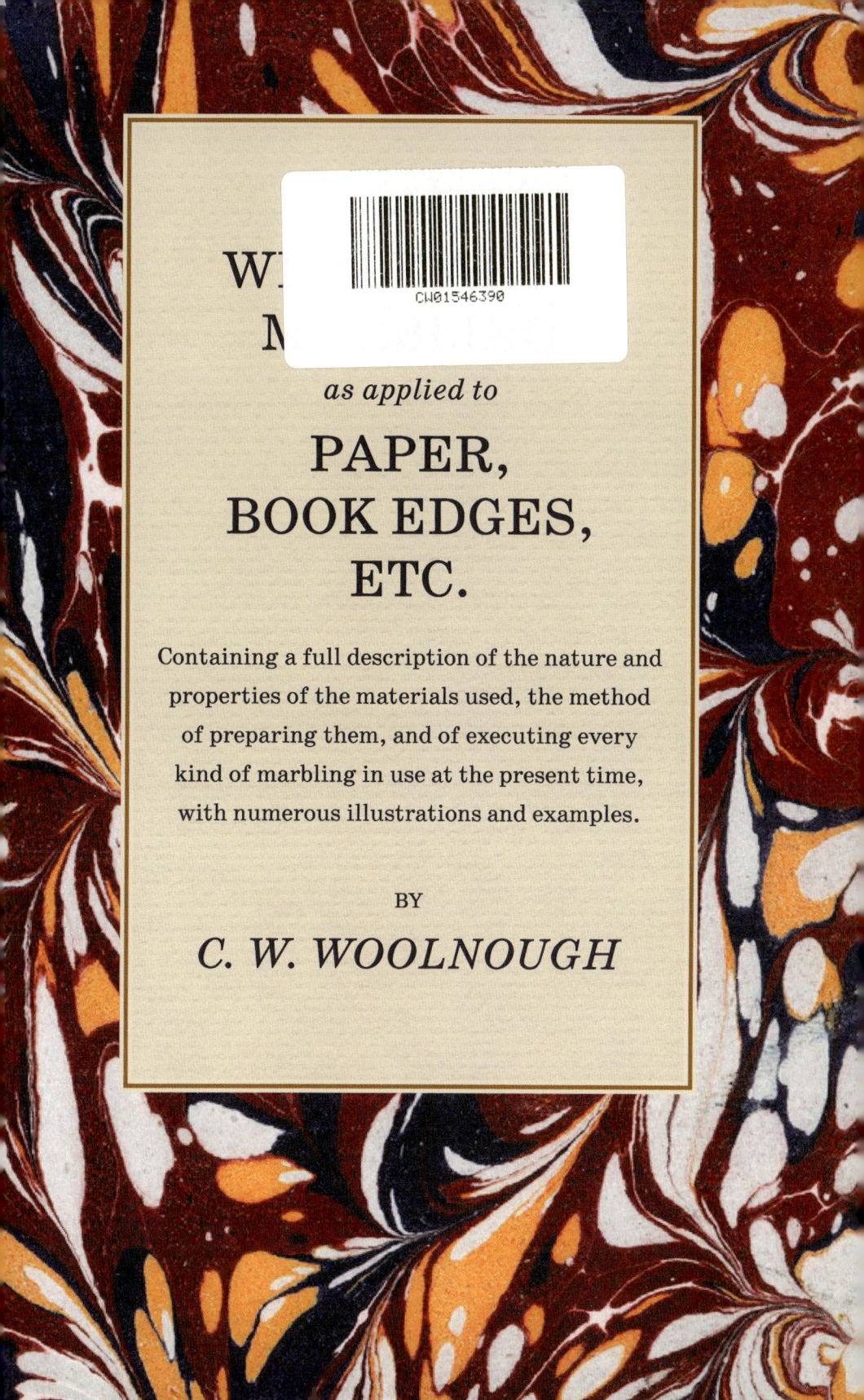

W[...]
M[...]

as applied to

PAPER,
BOOK EDGES,
ETC.

Containing a full description of the nature and properties of the materials used, the method of preparing them, and of executing every kind of marbling in use at the present time, with numerous illustrations and examples.

BY

C. W. WOOLNOUGH

Originally published in 1881, this edition, excluding Publisher's Note and annotations, is in the public domain and has been reproduced without any claim of copyright to the original work.

[SPG]

Published by Six Penny Graphics.
Fredericksburg, Virginia

2019 Publishers Note and annotations
© 2019 Six Penny Graphics.

ISBN: 978-1-7326595-1-3

This little work is dedicated to the

memory of professor

MICHAEL FARADAY,

whose kind interest and notice of his first work

the author begs gratefully to

record.

CONTENTS

2019 Publisher's Note: A brief timeline ix

Preface to This Edition. xiii

Introduction 1

The Whole Art of Marbling 3
    The Colours used in Marbling. 3
    Gum 11
    Linseed or Flax Seed 12
    Flea Seed (Plantago) 12
    Irish or Carrageen Moss 13
    Ox Gall 13
    Oil 14
    Spirits of Turpentine 15
    Kerosine, Paraffin, or Rock Oil 15
    Alum 15
    Water 16
    Of the Preparations or Vehicles Required for Marbling 16
    Of Grinding the Colours 16
    To Prepare the Wax for Grinding 17
    Troughs 17

Combs	18
The Arrangement of the Trough and Colours, etc	21
Sizing the Paper after Marbling	22
Glazing	22
Examples	23
Example No. 1	25
Example No. 2	29
Example No. 3	33
Example No. 4	37
Example No. 5	39
Example No. 6	41
Example No. 7	43
Example Nos. 8, 9, 10	47
Examples Nos. 11 and 12	51
Example No. 13	55
Examples Nos. 14, 15	57
Examples Nos. 16, 17	59
Examples Nos. 18, 19	63
Examples Nos. 20, 21, 22, 23	65
Example No. 24	77
Examples Nos. 25, 26, 27, 28, 28a, 29	79
Example No. 30	87
Example No. 31	91

Book Edges 93

Vellum or Stationery Work 97

Antique (Complex). 99

On the Adaptation of this Art for the
Manufacture of Paper-Hangings 101

Marbled Cloth 103

The Art of Marbling 105
    Transcript of Woolnough's lecture given before the *Journal of the Society of Arts* in 1878.

Index 117

2019 PUBLISHER'S NOTE: A BRIEF TIMELINE

All footnotes in this chapter have been added by the editor. In later chapters, footnotes from the original text are differentiated from the editor's by the insertion of the author's initials in red, i.e., **CWW**.

1853	*The art of marbling: as applied to book edges and paper, containing full instructions for executing British, French, Spanish, Italian, Nonpareil, etc., etc. Illustrated with specimens. With a brief notice of its recent application to textile fabrics, and particularly to the cloths so extensively used by bookbinders,* by Charles W. Woolnough, was published by Alexander Heylin in London.[1]
1854	*The Publishers' Circular*[2] included the following listing for Woolnough's books: CHEAP EDITION THE ART OF MARBLING as applied to BOOK-EDGES and PAPER: containing Full Instructions for executing all kinds of Marbling: with specimens. Also Brief Notice of its recent Application to Textile Fabrics. By C. W. WOOLNOUGH, Manager of the Patent Marbled Cloth Manufactory. 5s. Also, Just published by the same Author, HISTORY and DESCRIPTION of the PROCESS of MARBLING, as introduced into a lecture at the Royal Polytechnic Institution, Regent Street, by J. H. PEPPER, Esq. Royal 32mo. gilt edges, 6d. Alexander Heylin (late R. Baynes), 28, Paternoster Row.

1 WorldCat. http://www.worldcat.org/title/art-of-marbling-as-applied-to-book-edges-and-paper-containing-full-instructions-for-executing-british-french-spanish-italian-nonpareil-etc-etc-illustrated-with-specimens-with-a-brief-notice-of-its-recent-application-to-textile-fabrics-and-particularly-to-the-cloths-so-extensively-used-by-bookbinders/oclc/19530361&referer=brief_results (Accessed September 12, 2018.)

2 *Publishers' Circular and General Record of British and Foreign Literature.* London. April 1, 1854. p. 160.

1854	J.H. Pepper gave a lecture on the "Chemistry of the Manufacture of paper, and its Decoration with Colours, including Woolnough's Marbling Process" at the Royal Polytechnic Institution in London[3]
1854	A second edition was published.[4]
1878	The January 25 issue of the *Journal of the Royal Society of Arts*[5] carried a transcript of a paper entitled "The Art of Marbling" that was presented by C. W. Woolnough. This paper is reproduced here, beginning on page 105.
1878	In April of the same year, *Scientific American*[6] printed Woolnough's paper in its Supplement.
1881	*The Whole Art of Marbling as Applied to Paper, Book Edges, etc.* was published by G. Bell in London. The Metropolitan Museum of Art calls this 82-page edition, "The most important book on British marbling."[7]
1885	*The Royal Cornwall Gazette, Falmouth Packet, and General Advertiser*[8] wrote, A very interesting lecture on the art of marbling paper with numerous experiments was given in Cusgarne Schoolroom on Tuesday Evening by Mr. Woolnough.

---

3 The *Morning Post*. London. February 13, 1854.
4 World Cat. http://www.worldcat.org/title/art-of-marbling-as-applied-to-book-edges-and-paper-containing-full-instructions-for-executing-british-french-spanish-italian-nonpariel-sic-etc-etc/oclc/9950217&referer=brief_results (Accessed September 12, 2018.)
5 Woolnough, C. W. "The Art of Marbling." *Journal of the Royal Society of Arts*, January 25, 1878.
6 Woolnough. C. W. "The Art of Marbling." *Scientific American Supplement No. 119*, April 13, 1878.
7 https://www.metmuseum.org/art/collection/search/591856
8 "Gwennao Notes." The *Royal Cornwall Gazette, Falmouth Packet, and General Advertiser*, December 24, 1885.

1893 | An article in the *Royal Cornwall Gazette, Falmouth Packet, and General Advertiser*[9] reported the following:

> There is living in a humble cottage at Perranwell, says a correspondent of the *Western Daily Mercury*, an old gentleman of considerable literary, artistic, and scientific attainments. Mr. C. W. Woolnough, the gentleman in question, was the author of a book entitled "The Whole Art of Marbling," containing a full description of the nature and properties used, the method of preparing them, and of executing every kind of marbling in use at the present time, with numerous illustrations and examples. Previous to the publication of this work he, as a member of the Society of Arts, read a paper on the subject before the members in January 1878, Lieutenant-Colonel Sir E. F. Du Cane, K.C.B., R.E., in the chair. The lecture was listened to with the greatest interest, and highly commented on by those taking part in the discussion at its close. The paper is published in the journal of the Society of Arts, January 25th, 1878.

---

9 "Local Gossip." The *Royal Cornwall Gazette, Falmouth Packet, and General Advertiser*, August 10, 1893.

PREFACE TO THIS EDITION

More than twenty-seven years have now elapsed since the author submitted his first work to the notice of the bookbinding fraternity and the public in general, and the very favourable reception accorded to it, and in some instances, from quarters whence it was least expected, coupled with the fact that it has been for some years out of print (numerous applications having been made for copies without success), have induced the author once more to come forward with another edition, superior in every respect to the first, inasmuch as, while it contains all the matter supplied in the former, it possesses much additional information, embodying the results of the study, practice, and personal experience of considerably more than half a century, arranged in the most simple, progressive, and easy manner, calculated to develop the various processes of this "pretty, mysterious art," step by step, till nothing but practice will be required to make the student perfect.

As this is most probably the last time the author will intrude upon the notice of the public, he wishes to state that much time, labour and study, have been devoted to the object of rendering this work as perfect as possible, and worthy of still more extensive patronage among those who desire reliable information on this hitherto dubious and mystified subject, and he embraces the present opportunity of tendering his sincere thanks to those who so kindly, voluntarily, and encouragingly testified their interest in, and commendation of his book, among whom he feels proud to record the names of the late Professor Faraday, Professors Pepper, Bachhoffner, Dr. Normandy, and others; but perhaps as strong an evidence of the truthfulness and practical utility of the work as can be obtained from the encomiums of some, may be deduced from the hostility and bitterness of others, who, in the mistaken idea that their secrets were revealed, their rights invaded, and their pecuniary interest endangered, have given vent to their spleen by heaping upon him a variety of abuse, contumely, annoyance, and persecution. However, as he never had the least particle of instruction, information, or help of any kind from any of them (in fact, the majority of those who bear the names of masters possess but a very limited amount of knowledge of the principles and practice of the profession, and still less ability to impart it), he considers that he has an indisputable right to make use of the knowledge he has acquired by dearly bought experience and labour as he may deem proper. The author was also honoured (though with what motives he will leave others to guess) by our worthy transatlantic brethren, who reprinted it in Philadelphia and published it there in conjunction with some work on bookbinding. Not content with the benefit which might accrue to them in their own territory, they imported a quantity into this country and began to circulate them in London, obliging the author to institute proceedings for infringement of copyright.

But notwithstanding all these drawbacks, the interest which was manifested in this novelty was proved by the fact that not less than one hundred lectures, illustrated by experiments, were delivered at the Royal Polytechnic Institution, at Eton College, at some of the nobility's conversaziones, also before the late lamented Prince Consort and the late King of Portugal at a conversazione of the Royal Society at Connaught House, his Royal Highness manifesting great interest, and even condescending to try some experiments with his own hands, and carrying away with him a copy of the book.

There is one circumstance more which may be alluded to, for, whilst rather amusing, it serves to prove the truth of the foregoing statements, and must be admitted to be a testimony in favour of the work. Traveling through one of our large manufacturing towns or cities, the author was entering a house of business to solicit orders, when his attention was directed to an individual who was just leaving. As he passed out, the principal asked the question, "Do you know that man?" On replying in the negative, he remarked, in a bantering tone, "Why he is one of your fraternity, a most clever fellow, according to his own account he can do everything, and has published a book which tells you all about it for the small charge of sixpence; we shall soon be able to do without you altogether, and be 'Every man his own Marbler.'" On the following morning, proceeding through a bye-street, whom should he see but this very person, looking intently into the window of a tobacco shop with an empty pipe in his hand, and, as it was obvious that he was not too well off, he felt a little commiseration for him, and accosting him said, "Well, friend, were you not in such a place yesterday?" "Indeed I was," said he, putting the tip of his little finger into the bowl of his pipe, and then tapping it on the palm of his other hand, "but I don't remember seeing you there." "Never mind," was the reply, "I saw you, and was informed what a clever fellow you were. Now I sometimes do a little in that way myself; have you met with any success?" "Ah no," said he, "I have been on the tramp these ten days, worn the shoes off my feet walking from place to place in search of employment; no luck anywhere; shall leave here tonight and push on towards Liverpool." On a trifle being slipped into his hand, his countenance brightened, and with an exclamation of surprise, "Gad," said he, "but you are the best fellow I've met for many a long day," and, thrusting a hand into his coat pocket, he drew therefrom a small pamphlet of a few pages, saying, "Here, take this, there's something in it worth trying; I've tried it and proved it myself, and I can confidently recommend it to you; it's first-rate. I took it out of a half-guinea book published by one Woolnough of London; it's worth all the money." I never saw the poor fellow again, and he never knew that it was Woolnough himself to whom he had been confessing his delinquency, and at the same time so strongly recommending his own production.

It may not be out of place here to relate, by way of illustration, a circumstance which is calculated to throw a little light on the causes which have tended, in some measure, to cramp the progress of this art, and to discourage the development of its resources. Masters take lads as apprentices, engaging to teach them the Art and Mystery of Marbling, to whom it is a perfect mystery in every respect; these masters, in fact, possessing little or no knowledge of the practical or experimental working of the various and intricate processes connected with the successful carrying out of their object, and, as a rule, these lads are handed over to the tender mercies of the men employed, and, unless they are gifted with a little more than ordinary acuteness and penetration, will be kept in the dark as much as possible with regard to many things essential to their advancement and ultimate perfection in their calling. The case I now introduce will not exactly apply to the master, but only to the hands employed. In the beginning of the present century, a person possessing a general knowledge of the art as it was practised in those days devised a plan by which he acquired a moderate competency and retired in comfortable circumstances. The course adopted by him was the following. He took some half-dozen or more boys from the parish workhouse, and selecting such as appeared likely to suit his purpose, had them bound as apprentices. These lads he carefully trained, each to a separate class of work; for instance, he would keep one upon large French or Shell, another on the small, another on Italian, another to certain patterns of Spanish, and so on, bringing each to excel on a few patterns, but not making them perfect in all, with the exception of one, whom he required to do book edges, and for him it was necessary he should be taught the whole, he, as a matter of course, having higher wages than the others. Although at first there was a good deal of imperfect work produced, yet at that time prices were such as would amply remunerate for disposing of the produce of these embryo workers at a reduced price, and as they improved every week, while the cost for labour was so small, he soon found that his speculation was successful, and by the time these youths were out of their time he was able to command one of the most extensive and best paying concerns going. If any dispute arose, and any one of these men left, he found a difficulty in obtaining work, not having a full knowledge of all, and he had to return to his old place. This state of things continued for some years, and when he died, the business, being divided among the men, who, being taken from an illiterate and humble class, were not equal to the responsibility, suffered it to decay, and it is now only as one of the things of the past, and in the present age almost forgotten except by a very few.

C. W. Woolnough

INTRODUCTION

The Art of Marbling is by no means a novel invention, although it has been kept in the dark and involved in a kind of mystery by those who practised it. When the author was young, it was almost an impossibility for anyone, especially if they were at all connected with the bookbinding or stationery trades, to get a sight of the inside of the apartment where the process was performed, every hole and crevice through which you might get a peep was carefully stopped up, and "No Admission" put upon the door. However, patience and perseverance conquer difficulties, of which truth the work now before you is a witness; it is the only practical work of the kind that has ever appeared (except the smaller edition of twenty-seven years ago), calculated to impart correct instructions to the minds of those who desire to become acquainted with its various details. There have been many receipts given and articles written and printed in Cyclopaedias and works of a similar character, but the methods therein described are so utterly ridiculous that anyone possessing the smallest amount of knowledge on the subject must treat them with contempt. Marbling is an art which consists in the production of certain patterns and effects by means of colours so prepared as to float on a preparation of mucilaginous liquid which must possess properties of an antagonistic nature to those prepared colours, and which colours, while floating upon the surface of this mucilaginous liquid, are formed into patterns and taken off or transferred to a sheet of paper by gently laying the paper down upon it, or to the smoothly cut edges of a book by gently dipping it therein. This process is not very easy to describe, and yet to anyone beholding it for the first time it appears extremely simple and easy to perform, yet the difficulties are many and the longer anyone practises it, the more he becomes convinced that there is ample room for fresh discoveries and more interesting results than any that have yet been accomplished.

When it was first discovered, and by whom, or in what country it was first practised, it is hardly possible to determine. The old Dutch paper is not unfrequently found on books printed at the beginning of the seventeenth century, and circumstances seem to point to Holland or some locality near to that country as the place where it was then practised. Many years ago this old Dutch paper, generally in the size of foolscap, used to be imported into England, and in order to evade the duty to which it would be subject as an article of commerce, some of it (I do not mean to say all) was wrapped round small packages of Dutch toys, and thus as wrappers passed free, after which it was carefully taken off, smoothed out, and sold to the bookbinders at a good price for the better class of work; indeed, so choice was it, that in some of those old books the inside linings were formed of pieces neatly and cleverly joined together, and the brightness and durability of the colours after the lapse of so many years were surprising, while the execution of some of the antique specimens was no less so.

The question now before us is not how, when, or where it was first discovered, or practised, but to show as clearly and simply as possible how it is done or practised now, and to describe in a lucid, progressive, and comprehensive style the way in which the various patterns are manipulated, so that any individual possessing an ordinary share of common sense and understanding, may, without any other aid than practice, perseverance, and careful observation, do it himself, and where there are two ways of doing anything, that which half a century's experience has proved to be the best will be described. We will now proceed to describe, in the first place, the colours and materials used in Marbling.

THE WHOLE ART OF MARBLING

The Colours used in Marbling[1]

The colours required for this purpose are the same as those ordinarily used for painting either in oil or distemper,[2] but you must procure them just as they are produced or manufactured, whether in lump, powder, or pulp, and grind them yourself. They may be obtained in London retail at most of the respectable oil and colour shops, and in the provincial towns at the druggists, or wholesale at the principal colour manufacturers throughout the kingdom. I subjoin a list of all that are actually necessary, though many more may be brought into use to please the fancy.

Reds	Blues
Carmine.	Indigo.
Drop Lake.	Chinese Blue.
Peach Wood Lake (pulp).[3]	Prussian Blue.
Vermilion.	Ultramarine.
Rose Pink.	
Burnt Oxford Ochre.	

---

1 An excellent resource for information about the colors used can be found in the following book:
Thorpe, Edward, Sir. *A Dictionary of Applied Chemistry*, Volume IV. London: Longmans, Green, and Co., 1913.
2 *Distemper* – decorative paint using a binder of animal or vegetable origin (excluding egg).
3 cww: Made expressly for marbling.

Yellows	Browns
Chrome.	Burnt Turkey Amber.
Dutch Pink.[4]	Burnt Sienna.
Raw Oxford Ochre.	
Yellow Lake (pulp).	Orange
English Pink.[5]	Orange Lead
	Orange Chrome.
Greens	
Chrome Green.	Whites
Green Lake.	China Clay.
Emerald Green.	Pipe Clay.
Brunswick Green.	Flake White.
	Paris White.
Blacks	
Vegetable Lamp Black.	
Common Lamp Black.	
Drop Ivory Black.	
Blue Black.	

Carmine

This colour takes the first place among the reds for brilliancy of colour, and when properly ground and prepared is easy and sure to work, but it is seldom used on account of its high price; where, however, a little extra outlay is not an object, it amply repays for the additional expense by the superior lustre and permanency of the effects produced.

---

4 merriam-webster.com. www.merriam-webster.com/dictionary/ "Dutch Pink."
   1: a yellow lake prepared usually from Persian berries or from quercitron and used chiefly as an artist's pigment
   2: a light yellow that is greener and slightly darker than jasmine and greener and stronger than average maize or popcorn — called also *English pink, Italian pink, madder yellow, stil-de-grain yellow, yellow madder*

5 Ibid.

Drop Lake

Next to carmine, this is the most beautiful colour for book edges and is most generally used, especially for the Dutch or stationery marbling. There are three different sorts of this colour, viz. scarlet, crimson, and purple, and different qualities of each. The scarlet is best adapted for general purposes, as it possesses a greater brilliancy than the others; but as there is a great deal of a very inferior kind of drop lake about, which is of no use whatever to a marbler, possessing no body when ground and mixed, it will be as well to observe the following rule when about to purchase this article. Take a piece of the colour, break it, and apply the broken part to your tongue; if it adheres to your tongue like starch, reject it, as it is extremely doubtful whether it will do, but if it holds up the moisture without manifesting any disposition to adhere you may try it with better expectations of success, although this is not an infallible test. This colour is sold in the form of small cones or drops, from which it derives its name; it is a preparation of cochineal[6], therefore the cost of it depends much upon the price of that article.

Vermilion[7]

This colour is but little used, on account of its great specific gravity, and seldom without being combined with some other colour. It is a preparation of mercury, and though nominally a much lower price than lake, yet as so little of it in bulk goes to a pound it comes as dear or dearer than that article; it is, however, a permanent colour.

---

6   Thorpe says of processing Cochineal:
    "*Carmine* is the most important example of a lake pigment belonging to the first of these classes. The dried females of the cochineal insect, *Coccus cacti*, arc boiled with water, alum, stannous chloride and sodium carbonate being added. After standing for a few days, the decanted liquid throws down the pigment as a crimson precipitate, which is washed and dried."

7   Thorpe says of *Vermilion*:
    "*Vermilion, Cinnabar*, HgS (moderately permanent in oil: alterable in watercolour): too expensive for use in ordinary paints."

Peach Wood Lake

This colour is a preparation from peach wood and has only been introduced some twenty or thirty years to the general notice of the trade. It was first brought under my notice by Mr. Thos. Hinks[8], of Small Heath, Birmingham, manufacturer of colours, chemicals, etc., and is a great acquisition to the marbler, not only of book edges but also of paper, as the very reasonable price and superiority of appearance give it the advantage over all the common reds formerly used in the marbling of paper. This colour is an exception to the general rule, as it is sold in the pulp, or damp state, and may be mixed and even used without grinding, being manufactured almost exclusively for marbling; it is decidedly the best and cheapest red we have for general purposes; it possesses depth, permanence, and brilliancy, and ranks next to drop lake. It may be necessary to state that it is not known at the druggists or colour shops, but must be obtained only from the maker, Mr. Hinks[9, 10, 11], who for the convenience of all parties requiring it, will supply it in either large or small quantities. [12]

Rose Pink

This is a very useful though common colour for paper; it is made by boiling chalk or whiting in a decoction of Brazil wood. It is a very fugitive colour, the pink very quickly fading on exposure to the atmosphere or to heat. Combined with a little orange lead or burnt ochre, it answers for a

---

8   Thomas Hinks and Sons were "Colour and Chemical Manufacturers" and were also involved with the production of mercury fulminate.
    "Public Notices." *The Birmingham Daily Post*. September 12, 1885.
9   There was a large explosion of two to three pounds of mercury fulminate in Hinks' factory in 1859. It was reported that, "Fragments of brick and slate from the manufactory strewed gardens four hundred yards distant."
    "Another Explosion of Fulminate of Mercury." *The Birmingham Daily Post*. December 26, 1859.
10 Nine people were killed and thirty injured in a gun cap factor when mercury fulminate supplied by Hinks exploded.
    "Fearful Catastrophe." *The Birmingham Daily Post*. June 23, 1862.
11 A second explosion occurred in 1876. One man was killed. "The Fatal Explosion at Small Heath." *The Birmingham Daily Post*. May 31, 1876.
12 *Woolnough:* Since writing this I find other makers of this colour in the market.

vein colour for common paper, or mixed with indigo or Chinese blue it makes a good purple.

Burnt Ochre

This colour is obtained in its raw or native state from pits dug in the earth in the neighbourhood of Oxford, hence it is called Oxford ochre, and from its hardness, especially when burnt, "stone ochre." It is a sort of clay, and when burnt or made red-hot, turns to a kind of red colour; it is one of the most useful colours we have, and as the price is low is extensively used. With the addition of a little black it makes a good brown, with a little blue or indigo it makes a good olive, and is a good bright fawn colour when used by itself, and is not liable to fade or change.

Chinese Blue

This is a very beautiful, but not a very durable colour; it is, however, an almost indispensable one to the marbler, as it will produce nearly every shade of blue by the addition of certain proportions of white. This colour requires particularly well grinding, as indeed do all the blues; it is also sold in some places in the pulp or damp state, both deep and pale.

Indigo

This colour is a most valuable article, and cannot be dispensed with under any consideration. The East India or Bengal is the best. It is too well known to require any description here. Though not a bright colour, it is one of the most durable; and for mixing and producing greens and purples of a permanent kind is invaluable, neither can you make a good black without it; but be sure you obtain it good.

Ultramarine

This is a very beautiful colour, but must be used very sparingly, as it will not glaze or take any polish, and is always inclined to rub off. The kinds now in general use are the French and German, the genuine article being far too expensive for this sort of work.

Prussian Blue

This colour is now almost superseded by the Chinese blue, which is a much brighter colour; Prussian blue is much darker and heavier-looking than the Chinese, and is a very bad colour for glazing, and harder to grind.

Dutch Pink[13]

This is a common but very useful colour; it is a preparation of whiting and Quercitron bark. Mixed with blue or indigo, it makes a good green, and is also useful in mixing with chrome to produce the various shades of yellow you may require.

English Pink

This is sometimes useful, it contains only half the depth of colour to be found in Dutch pink.

Yellow Lake[14]

A good colour for general purposes, principally used for old Dutch, and also for making greens mixed with blue.

Chrome (Pure)

There are various shades of this colour, known as lemon, middle, and orange, varying in shade from a pale lemon to a deep orange approaching red; it is a useful colour, but unless you get it pure or genuine, is very difficult to get to work properly.

Raw Ochre

Raw Ochre is Oxford ochre in its native state. This may be used in certain proportions for making your olive or stone-coloured tints combined with Dutch pink, white, blue, or black; it is also of use in small quantities to

---

13 Thorpe says::
 "…*yellow lake, brown pink, Italian pink, 'yellow madder,' Dutch pink, yellow carmine, citrine lake, 'stil de grain,' sap green, lokao (Chinese green)*, and other pigments, are derived from quercitron bark, *Quercus discolor* (Ait.), &c., or from different species of buckthorn (*Rhamnus*), including Persian, Avignon and other berries."

14 Ibid.

mix with your yellows when they are inclined to run off; this colour being of a very adhesive nature.

Drop Ivory Black[15]

This colour cannot be well used alone, it requires to be combined with lamp black and indigo to get it to work properly as a black.

Vegetable Black

This is a superior kind of lamp black, but made from vegetable instead of animal matter: it is surprisingly light and cannot be used alone. It will not produce a good black for marbling except in combination with double its own weight of good indigo. A little drop black may be used with it.

Green

Most of the green colours used in marbling are produced by mixing certain proportions of Dutch pink or yellow lake with blue according to the shade required, which must be regulated by your own judgment. As to the blue used, it must be remembered that Chinese blue will fade (indigo will not), and should the green be inclined to run off, a little raw Oxford ochre will be necessary. There are many green colours sold at the colour shops: among them is the emerald green, but it is comparatively useless in marbling, as it possesses but little body and will not burnish, and being prepared from arsenic is a rank poison and injurious to health.

---

15   Thorpe says of various black pigments
    "Animal black, bone black (Beinschwarz), ivory black, Paris black, sugar house black. The first [Animal black] is obtained as the carbonaceous *residuum of* the destructive distillation of miscellaneous animal offal, the second [bone black]in a like manner from bones, and the third [ivory black]is or should be produced similarly from waste ivory. Ivory black—particularly when the lime salts have been removed by digestion in hydrochloric acid—is the most intense of the black pigments: it is stated… that lampblack will make a light mark on ivory black. The animal blacks exert considerable decolourising power when associated in an aqueous medium with organic colouring matters, hence they are more advisedly used in oils than for water-colour painting. Notably hygroscopic, such pigments should be dried before being ground in oil. *Soap black* is a form of ivory black moulded into pastilles with a little gum-water."

Brunswick Green

Brunswick green will not stand the light of the atmosphere, but will fade in a few hours; it is, however, a very cheap colour, but not adapted for marbling. The best of all the ready-made greens is good green lake.

Green Lake

Green lake is a deep bright colour, and more permanent than the others, but too expensive for paper. Next to this comes the chrome green.

Chrome Green[16]

Chrome green also a pretty good colour. But it is hardly worth while to multiply these, as it will only tend to confuse rather than to edify the learner.

Turkey Umber Burnt

This colour produces a very good brown, but it is hardly needed, as it requires a great deal of grinding and requires to lie some time after to soften or rot, while if you have the burnt Oxford ochre, with the aid of indigo and black you can produce almost any shade of brown you may require.

Orange Lead[17]

This is a very heavy colour, and is mostly used for the edges of account books; it may, however, be used in the manufacture of marbled paper, but

---

16   Thorpe says of *chrome green*:
  "*Chrome green*.... Prepared by (*a*) igniting ammonium dichromate, (*b*) igniting mercurous dichromate, (*c*) heating together potassium chromate and sulphur, (*d*) the ignition of a mixture of potassium dichromate, ammonium chloride, and sodium carbonate. This fine pigment is... either approximately pure, anhydrous chromium sesquioxide,...or... chromium phosphate... Some products are a mixture of the two compounds. The oxide pigments are of finer hue than the phosphate colours. Chrome green is one of the most permanent, generally trustworthy, and widely applicable colours used by artists."

17   Thorpe says of *orange lead:*
  "*Red lead, Orange lead, minium, mennige, Paris red,...* , a fine orange-red pigment, which very quickly dries in oil but is discoloured by sulphuretted hydrogen, and is incompatible in admixture with certain sulphur-containing pigments, such as lithopone and cadmium yellow... *Orange mineral* is a less dense form of red lead."

a large proportion of it will sink to the bottom of the trough on account of great weight.

White

For this an article called China clay is mostly used; also, for some purposes, common pipeclay will answer. Flake white may also be used, but it is much heavier, and the others do quite as well and are much cheaper. Paris white is a similar thing to the china clay, but harder, and is apt to clog the brushes, as it is often mixed with plaster of Paris.

Gum

Of all the varieties of gum, there is but one that is of any use for the purpose of marbling, and that is called gum tragacanth, or gum dragon—called by some druggists gum elect. You cannot be too particular in your choice of this article, on which so much of the excellence of your work depends. It is like the foundation of a building: if that be faulty, the whole fabric will fall to the ground. Good gum should be large, white, hard, and flaky (although I have occasionally had some very good in small white flakes), but that which is discoloured and lumpy is doubtful, it is no gain to buy it, however cheap it may be offered; if used at all, it would only do for the most common kinds of work, and even then one pound of the best would go farther than two of the bad and produce a more satisfactory result. Have the best of everything, and it will be cheapest in the end, as the loss of time, joined with the inferiority of the work produced by the use of bad material, will prove. Good gum will produce a smooth surface when dissolved, but bad gum will often yield a rough one, which is inimical to your purpose. Again, some apparently good gum, or gum which has been exposed some time to the action of the atmosphere, will give a smooth surface enough, and yet possess no strength; the colours will flow well, and form themselves properly, and, when the paper is lifted off, will look at first very beautiful; but upon looking at it after it has been hanging up for five minutes, you will find the colours all running off, to your indescribable annoyance and vexation.

Directions for preparing the Gum

Procure a large earthen pan, glazed on the inside, capable of holding from eight to twelve gallons; put therein one pound of gum tragacanth, and pour on it about two gallons of soft water; let it soak all night. The next morning stir it up well with a birch broom for about five minutes, breaking the lumps; repeat this at intervals of three or four hours during the day, adding more water as it thickens, or absorbs that which was first put to it. In about forty-eight hours you may venture to make use of it, though seventy-two hours would be better, and I have found some gum which worked all the better for remaining a week in solution, as, although a considerable portion of the gum may be dissolved, some of the hardest pieces, which contain the most valuable properties of the gum, will still remain in a semi-solid state. When your gum is properly dissolved, you must gradually dilute it with water till it is brought to the proper consistency, when it must be strained through a fine hair or muslin sieve. If you require it for Nonpareil, you must be particularly careful that you have no lumps in it, or they will get between the teeth of your comb and drag the colours; if for Spanish or Shell, it will require to be rather thinner than for Nonpareil, and if for the old Dutch or Account Book pattern a little thicker; but a little practice will soon enlighten the practitioner on this part of the process.

Linseed or Flax Seed

It is possible to marble some common patterns on mucilage of linseed alone, but it is a very objectionable vehicle for more reasons than one. If used, the linseed must either be boiled, or boiling water must be poured upon it, and kept stirred for a considerable time, to extract the mucilage from the seed; but it is very seldom used, as it so quickly decomposes, or turns to water.

Flea Seed (Plantago)

This is an article but little known except by those who have occasion to use it; its peculiar appellation arises, I suppose, from its great similarity to the very annoying little insect whose name it bears, being very like it in shape, colour, and size. When saturated with boiling water, and well stirred, it will yield when cold a very strong and powerful mucilage, far stronger than what can be obtained from linseed; and, what is better still, it will not soon lose its properties, or turn to water, but will keep good for days. It is a great improvement when mixed with the gum for the making of the French or Spanish marbles; but it is a total enemy to Nonpareil and all drawn patterns, as it will not allow a comb to pass through it without dragging all the colour off with it. To prepare it for use, put a quarter of a pound of seed into a pan or crock, pour upon it a gallon of boiling water, keep it well stirred for ten minutes, let it stand for half an hour, then stir it again for ten minutes more. In another half-hour pour a second gallon of boiling water, stirring it as before, at intervals, for one hour. Let it remain, and the seed will settle at the bottom of the vessel; when cold, pour off the top for use, and the seed will bear more boiling water, though not so much as at first. And sometimes the seed will yield a third supply; but this you must determine by your own judgment, as the seed when exhausted will lose its mucilaginous property, and must then be thrown away. One thing I would mention—never stir your seed up after it is cold, or nearly so, or it will not settle again without being heated afresh, or more boiling water being added to it, and it would be very difficult to strain it.

Irish or Carrageen Moss

This may be either used or let alone; some like to use a little of it mixed with the gum for Nonpareil. It must be well washed and soaked in cold water, and be gently boiled for an hour or two, and when cold, strained, and well beaten up with the gum before putting it into the trough. But do not attempt to use it either for Spanish or French, as it will do more harm than good. It is possible to marble on this alone also.

Ox Gall

The surest way of obtaining this article genuine is by procuring it in the bladder as it comes from the animal, if you are acquainted with any butcher on whom you can depend; if not, you must ascertain that the bag or bladder has not been broken, as I have been deceived myself in this way. I will here expose the method of the fraud practised on me. I had for some time been supplied with galls from a slaughter-house, but finding that although, the galls were brought in the skins, and emptied into a jar in my presence, it took a great deal to produce the proper effect, I set my thoughts to work to find out the cause, and at last discovered that the man who brought them procured one or two good galls, and at the same time obtained some empty bags or skins from which the gall had been taken; he then mixed the genuine with a quantity of water, and refilled the whole lot, carefully tying them up with a fine string, and selling them to me as the proper article. The gall from some animals is very thick and ropy; but, if kept awhile, will go thin, without losing its properties. In fact, gall is all the better for being kept some time, and is none the worse for stinking, excepting the disagreeableness of the odour to those using it.

Oil

This is an agent of which you cannot be too careful, for, although it is indispensable for the production of some patterns, it is a most formidable enemy to the perfect accomplishment of others; indeed, a brush which has been used in the colour mixed for a French or Shell pattern, would, if put into a jar of colour in use for Spanish or Nonpareil, completely spoil it for those purposes, unless it were thoroughly cleansed from every particle of grease. I just mention this to show the necessity of being most scrupulously particular in everything connected with the processes of marbling, and how apparently trifling a matter may throw an obstacle in the way such as you would hardly credit.

Now the best oil for general use in French or Shell marbles is the Florence or olive oil. It may be had in flasks at most druggists' or Italian warehouses. Other oils may be used, such as linseed or boiled oil; but for general purposes the olive is best, and least trouble to work.

Spirits of Turpentine

This is also another agent which requires to be kept under careful control, as it will make your colour full of holes and blotches where they are not wanted.

Kerosine, Paraffin, or Rock Oil

This is another extraordinary production of nature, only of recent introduction. Little can be said about it at present, but it appears to partake somewhat of the properties, and to produce something of the effects of spirits of turpentine, and if used must be used with caution. However, if any have time and inclination to experiment, let them do so, as, in this way, novel and, it may be, important results may be attained.

Alum

This is a well-known substance, of a light colour, and a sharp acid taste, soluble in boiling water; but although you may keep it dissolved while heated, if allowed to stand till cold, you will find only a certain proportion of the alum taken up by the water, the remainder forming itself into crystals at the bottom of the vessel; but if you pour the liquid off, and add more water, by repeating the process you may get it all dissolved. The uses to which this article may be applied in marbling are (first) to counteract the effect of too much gall in the colours. If any one of your colours should spread or run out too much, a few drops of this solution of alum will check it, and cause it to contract or close up, but it must be used with caution, as it will affect the tints of some colours, and will also resist the friction of the flint in glazing, causing it to tear.

Secondly, if put into the solution of gum tragacanth it will make it thicken, and help it to keep good a little longer; but it is not possible to work well with it, as it will only produce very inferior work. It takes a great deal more gall to make the colours flow out upon it, the one being opposed to the other; still, it is sometimes useful at a pinch, but it is better to do without it altogether if possible.

It is also a necessary ingredient in the making size for the paper after marbling.

There are, doubtless, other agencies at present hidden from us, which the light of advancing science and increasing knowledge will reveal, producing effects which may throw all our present attainments in the shade; but till then we must make the best use of the means within our reach, and by cultivating these we may reap more than we expect.

Water

Soft or rainwater, where it can be procured, is best adapted for all the preparations of marbling, but hard water will do, especially if a small quantity of soda or pearlash be dissolved in it. Water that has been boiled, and allowed to cool, answers every purpose.

Of the Preparations or Vehicles Required for Marbling

For Spanish, French, or Shell, Italian, West End, and British, you will require a mixture of the solution of gum tragacanth and the mucilage of flea-seed in the proportion of one quart of the latter to two gallons of the former; beat them well up together till they are thoroughly incorporated with each other, strain the mixture through the hair sieve into your trough, and it will be fit for use.

For Dutch, Nonpareil, Curl, Antique, and in short all patterns which require to be formed with any kind of instrument on the surface of the preparation in the trough, you had better use nothing but the pure solution of gum tragacanth; in fact, you may marble all the patterns on this alone, so that if you find any difficulty in procuring the other articles mentioned, if you can only procure good gum you may do any or all the varieties of marbling upon it, although some patterns are improved by the addition of the preparation of the flea-seed before described.

Of Grinding the Colours

On this point, you must be very particular, for if any of your colours are not finely or properly ground, you must not expect your work to look well. Where a large quantity of colour is required, a colour-mill is the most advantageous method to be adopted, but if on a small scale the ordinary slab and muller will answer the purpose; but whether by the mill or by hand, the colours must be ground perfectly smooth and fine. They must be all ground with a preparation of beeswax, in the proportion of one ounce of the prepared wax to one pound of colour; this will prevent the colour from rubbing off, and make it burnish or glaze easily.

To Prepare the Wax for Grinding

To attempt to grind beeswax in its native state would be a fruitless task, as it would only stick to the stone, and would not unite with the other ingredients. To obviate this you must prepare it in the following manner. Take of the very best beeswax (two pounds), put it in an earthen pipkin, and with it a quarter of a pound of the very best white curd soap[18], cut in very thin small pieces, place it in a gentle heat, and when both are quite dissolved (but be sure they are not boiling) put the pipkin containing the hot liquid on a table, taking in one hand a jug containing cold water, and gently stirring the wax with the other, pour in the water a little at the time, keeping it constantly stirred, and you will find it gradually thicken till at last you will hardly be able to stir it at all; but you must be very careful not to have it too hot when you pour in the water, for if you do the moment the water and wax come in contact it will fly up out of the pipkin, and perhaps scald you. Set it to cool, and when cold you will be able to pulverize it between your thumb and finger; in this state you may mix or grind it with the colour easily, but it is best if worked well in with the dry colour before you wet it.

Troughs

The troughs are generally made of wood and must be water-tight, and perfectly flat and smooth at bottom inside, because, where bottom combs are used, any unevenness would injure them, and be likely to distort the pattern. Sometimes they are made of slate, which is better; but they

---

18   A hard soap such as castile.

are very heavy, if you have to shift them, and are more expensive. With regard to sizes, some are made to take in a single sheet, others two sheets together; but whatever their size, they should be a little larger than the paper for Spanish, French, Italian, etc., but for Nonpareil and patterns of that class, it will require to be larger still, or the edges of the paper will be imperfect. There should be a small partition on the right-hand side, about three inches wide, made by letting in a narrow piece of wood or slate, about a quarter of an inch in thickness, and so placed in a sloping position,—the top being about an eighth of an inch below the sides,—as to allow of the waste being skimmed over it, without running over the sides. A hole about the size of a wine cork should be made in one corner, to run the contents out whenever you want to do so. A skimmer, constructed of a; thin piece of wood about three or four inches wide, and of sufficient length to pass along the inside of the trough without interruption, when drawn along the surface of the fluid for the purpose of skimming, will also be required, as it must be skimmed for every sheet made.

Combs

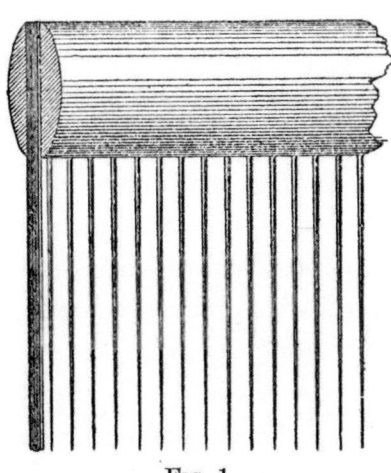

Fig. 1.

The combs used in marbling are various in their construction, some being what are termed top and others bottom combs; that is, one is drawn along the top of the fluid in the trough, the teeth just touching the floating colours, while the other is put to the bottom and held down with the points of the teeth touching the bottom of the trough all the time it is being drawn through. They should be made with brass wire, the smaller the pattern the finer the wire. See Fig. 1. The bottom combs are generally made by a reed-maker, that is, one who manufactures the peculiarly fine and uniformly regular wire apparatus used by the silk weavers in their business, and which they can divide with the nicest precision and exactness into any number of teeth to the inch; but twelve or thirteen to the inch is fine enough for any Nonpareil comb, if finer it is apt to drag.

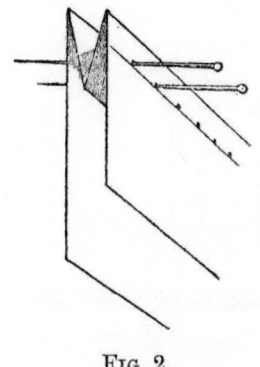

Fig. 2.

The top combs are generally manufactured by the parties using them, and various methods have been adopted for the purpose. Pins, needles, and wire have been brought into requisition, and with various results, according to the ingenuity or clumsiness of the individual attempting the task. The greatest difficulties are: first. keeping uniform distance or space between the teeth; second, keeping the points exactly level, so that they may touch the level surface of the liquid all over, without having one part under and another not touching at all; third, having them perfectly flat, not bent or crooked, one part inclined to stand out behind and another part sticking out before, as with these defects it will be impossible to produce a regular or uniform appearance. We will, therefore, try to describe to you a method which, after many years' practice and experience, we consider the most easy and most likely to be successful.

Cut some pieces of paper about four or five inches long and about two and a half broad, carefully, evenly, and exactly fold them as in Fig. 2, thus:—That is, fold it first nearly in half, then turn the widest part back and fold it evenly about one-eighth of an inch from the first fold, turn it back again level with the first fold; then draw a line parallel with the edge of the fold either with ink or pencil about one-twelfth of an inch from the edge, so as to permit the pins or needles to catch in the part folded back, and measure and mark out the distances through which your points are to be put. If you find any difficulty in comprehending this plan, purchase a sheet of pins and observe the manner in which they are stuck through, closing up the folds of the paper, and the idea will be realized at once. Some combs have been made of such pins, but the heads are in the way.

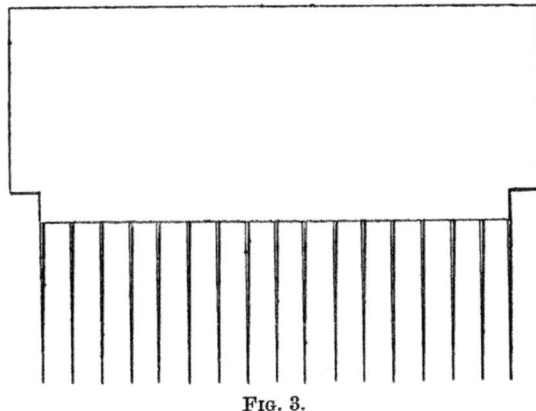

Fig. 3.

When you have stuck your needles or pins you will require to regulate them; if any have gone askew or you have any crooked ones, they must be replaced by others, and you must leave as much as possible of the length of the needles or pins from the points as you can do consistently with security for holding them fast in their places; and in order to do this you must flatten the paper out again, and with the side of a knife or something perfectly level, press against the points till they are quite even, then take a narrow strip of paper glued and secure them by sticking it on to the upper part, and when that is dry you can turn back the other part of the paper and with a little thin glue stick the two folds together: this will leave the points sticking out like a comb, and render it doubly secure. See Fig. 3. You can now fix any number of these short lengths upon a piece of thin wood, perfectly true and exact, two or three inches wide, as the size of your trough may require; taking care to trim the ends of each piece so that it shall join the other without making a gap between, and it will be necessary to cut a piece out of each end of the wood, permitting it to rest upon the edges of the trough, to allow of your guiding it evenly along. I here again observe that you must have the trough made very true and level in every part, for although the bottom combs may be made to work provided the bottom only be smooth and level, yet the top combs cannot be made to do unless the sides are level also. In order to test the level of the trough when the liquid is in it, take a piece of stick, or your finger, put it to the bottom of the liquid, in one part mark the depth; try another part in the same manner, till you get it the same depth all over. Should your table or bench be uneven, you must wedge it up by putting small wedge-shaped pieces of wood between the bottom of the trough and the table where it may be required; and you must be very particular in thus adjusting your trough, especially in those patterns which require combs or other instruments in their production.

In using the bottom comb it will be necessary to have a small trough, about a couple of inches in width and filled with clean water, on the left-hand side of the trough, in which to place the comb when you have drawn it through the colour, or it will get clogged. The combs must occasionally be brushed, as frequently little impediments will get between the teeth and make an unsightly mark through the sheet.

The Arrangement of the Trough and Colours, etc

Procure a firm level table, or fixed bench, of a convenient height, sufficiently large to hold your trough and leave you some feet of spare room on each side of it; you must place the pots or jars containing the colours on your right hand, and your paper or books to be marbled on your left. Have the gall-bottle handy; better place it between some of the jars, where it will not be likely to get knocked over, as you will be obliged to have frequent recourse to it, to keep your colours in good working order, as a very trifling matter will throw them out; fill your trough to within half or three-quarters of an inch of the top with your solution, whatever kind it may be, proceed to mix and try your colours, at first a few spots at the time, on the surface of the solution, adding the ingredients, as their effects may reveal to you the necessity thereof by their action and appearance, adjusting their proportions till you obtain the desired effects, and trying them on small pieces of paper before hazarding whole sheets. When you are satisfied that both solution and colours are in perfect order, skim the surface of the solution all over, taking care not to agitate it too much, commence sprinkling on the colours immediately, and then you can proceed as in the following examples.

Sizing the Paper after Marbling

This depends much upon the nature of the paper you have to size. If it be an ordinary hard-sized printing paper, the size will not need to be so strong as it would be for the proper half-sized paper made for the express purpose of marbling. The ordinary size is prepared as follows: Take half a pound of the best pale soap and half a pound of best glue. Cut the soap into small pieces, and boil them together in three gallons of water till dissolved. Then dissolve in another vessel half a pound of alum by boiling. Mix the two together in as near a boiling state as you possibly can, in a tub or any other vessel that will hold it, stirring them up well; and, when cool, put the preparation into a trough similar to those used for marbling, and lay the paper in it, just in the same manner, taking it out on a stick, and hanging it up to dry in the same way. If the paper be very soft, more glue may be used in making the size, after which it will be ready for glazing.

Glazing

This is accomplished by means of a machine similar to those used by calenderers to glaze prints and curtains and is effected by the friction of a smoothly surfaced flint stone on the face of the paper. We will endeavour to describe it. A polished or smoothly faced flint stone is fixed in a block of wood, having a handle at the centre of each side to work it by. Over the flint is fixed one end of a pole, about five feet long, the other end being placed in a hole or cavity in a spring board overhead, so as to allow the flint to be moved backwards and forwards at will, upon a piece of wood so hollowed out as to admit of an equal pressure all over; the longer the pole the less hollow the plank or block requires to be. It is very hard work by hand and is now mostly done by steam power. Some is done by heated steel cylinders, as bookbinders' cloth is done; but this is objectionable, as the paper is made very thin, and is more difficult to use, being apt to curl up when pasted, and difficult to keep from creasing and stretching.[19]

19 **cww:** It may be as well to observe that, of the examples of marbling that follow, the completed patterns are all glazed. Only those that illustrate the progress of a pattern are unglazed.

The Illustrative Examples in this Volume have been executed expressly for this work under the immediate superintendence of the Author, and most of them by his own hand.

✦

Example No. 1 — Blue Italian

EXAMPLE NO. 1

As gall is the principal acting ingredient in every pattern—in fact, as it is impossible to proceed without it—we will, in the first place, by the aid of a very simple pattern, endeavour to illustrate its effects.

Assuming, therefore, that you have the solution in the trough properly prepared, and of the right consistency, your colours ground as directed, and everything conveniently arranged and ready to hand, take two pots or jars, in one of these mix up a little blue colour with gall and water, and in the other a little gall and water alone: about half a table-spoonful of gall to half-a-pint of water will be about the proportion, but for this no exact rule can be given, as all galls are not of the same strength, the only way of determining this being by trying its effects on the solution, by sprinkling a few drops of the colour on it first; if it does not float or flow out and spread on the surface of the solution, you must add more gall, a little at a time, till you produce the appearance represented by the example (*a*, No. 1, page 27), then take the brush with the gall and water, and sprinkle it carefully and evenly over the blue you have just previously put on, and if you have the right proportion of gall in the water it will produce the effect represented in the example (*b*, No. 1): if there is not enough gall in the water it will only give the appearance of white spots on the blue; if too much, it will drive the blue up into very fine veins, leaving too much of the white paper exposed; this you will soon be able to rectify by a little judgment and practice. This example is given simply to illustrate the effects of gall, and to show how important a place it occupies in the production of the marvellous and beautiful varieties with which this book is illustrated.

But if, instead of sprinkling or throwing on the colours by the hand, you put them on by striking or knocking the stock of the brush against a small iron rod or bar about half an inch in thickness, you will have a neat network in lieu of the larger spots and coarse veins, and the pattern called Blue Italian (See No. 1, page 24) will be produced.

Size or medium: a mixture of gum tragacanth and flea-seed.

Example No. 1. [Blue Italian]

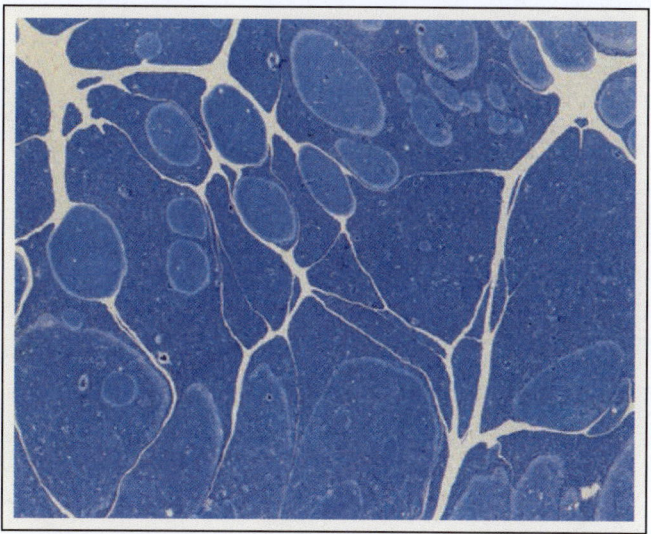

A

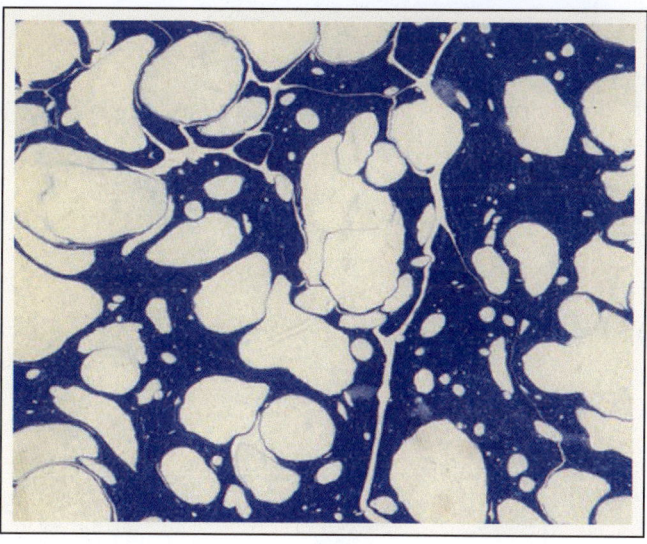

B

EFFECTS OF GALL AND WATER

EXAMPLE NO. 2

Italian Four Veins

We will now take the example no. 2. In this, you must adopt the same method of procedure, the only difference being a greater number of colours, and of course a little more difficulty in the manipulation. You will now require five jars and brushes, one for each colour (viz.), red, yellow, green, blue, and white, or gall and water; they must all be mixed with gall and water as in the preceding example, but each succeeding colour will require a little more gall than its predecessor, and the white, or last colour, must be sufficiently strong in gall to drive the other colour sup into very fine, small veins; you must expect to make several trials before you succeed in getting your colours all right for working. I have given progressive illustrations for your guidance by which you will see the changes which take place as each additional colour is sprinkled on the solution in the trough; you must begin with knocking on the red; secondly, yellow; thirdly, green; fourthly, blue; and the effects produced should be such as you will see marked *a, b, c, d, e*, in the illustrated example No. 2. These four colours may be put on with small brushes, but the white or gall and water will require a larger brush and should be held up on a level with your head and beaten on evenly all over the other colours; if you hold it low down near the surface you will produce a cloudy, irregular appearance, unsightly to the eye, and unfit for good work.

When well done it is a very neat and pretty, though simple pattern, but requires great carefulness and cleanliness in making or working, in order to turn it out well; and you must be very careful to keep the rings of the brushes wiped with a piece of rag after dipping them in the colour, before commencing to knock them against the iron rod, as the colour will accumulate on them and fall in large spots or blotches here and there, which will spoil the appearance of the work altogether.

Note, gall and water is preferable for the top colour for book edges, but you can work with more certainty, especially by gas or candlelight, by mixing a little white with it; all the colours for this pattern require to be thin.

Some are made with one colour only, such as red or blue; some with two, but the working is the same in all.

Size or medium: a mixture of gum tragacanth and flea-seed.

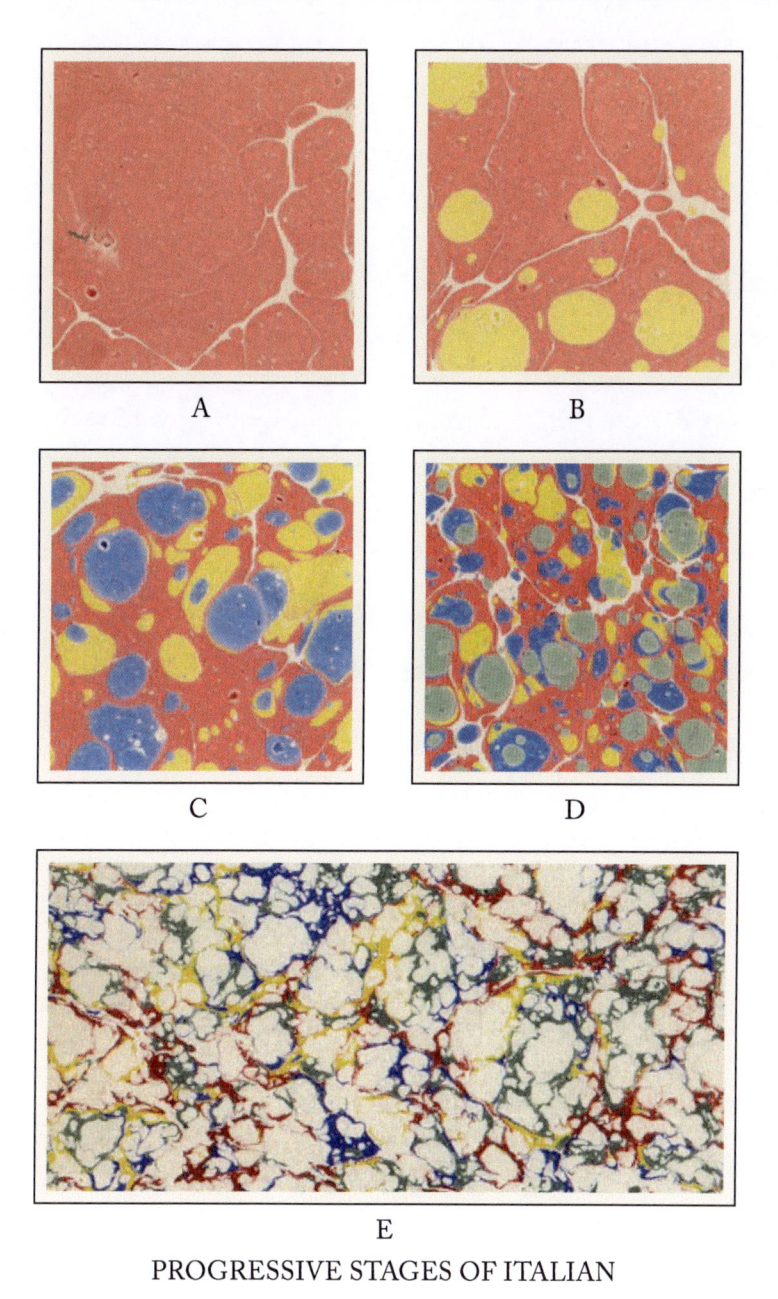

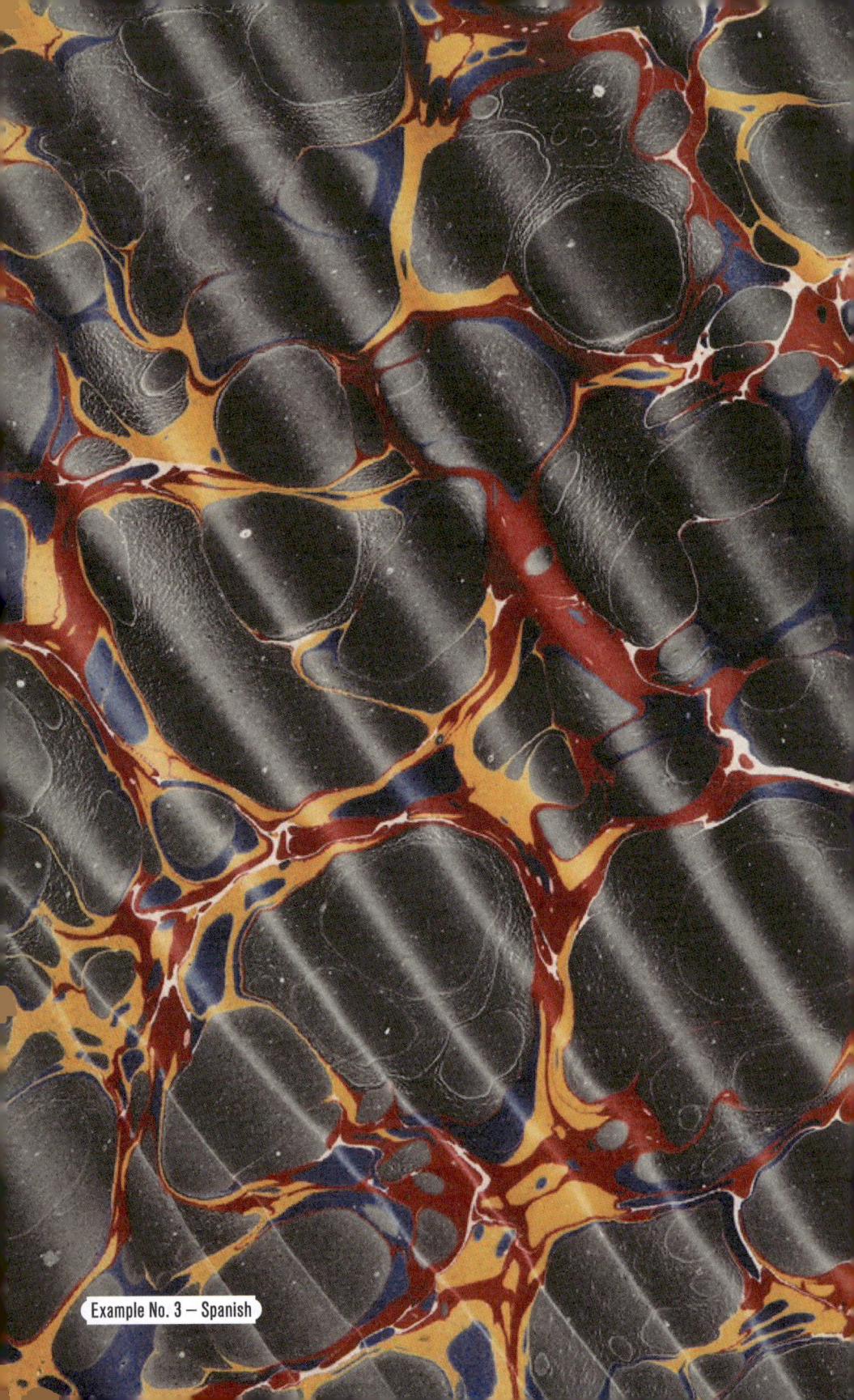
Example No. 3 – Spanish

EXAMPLE NO. 3

Spanish

You must not imagine that there is anything like nationality attached to any of these varieties of marbling on account of their names. England has long maintained, and still maintains the pre-eminence over every other country in this very peculiar and interesting branch of art industry. Many of the foreign papers are got up with a beautiful surface and finish while the intrinsic merit of the work is of a very mean standard, and are sold at a much cheaper rate than that at which they can be produced by the British workman. But to proceed. This sort of marbling is distinguished from all others by having a series of light and dark shades traversing the whole extent of the sheet of paper in a diagonal direction, and if you will closely follow the instructions here laid down, the striking beauty of the effects will not be more surprising than the simplicity of the method adopted for producing them. The colours for the veins may be mixed in the same manner as for the previous patterns, that is, with gall and water, and the same preparation of gum and flea-seed is used to work upon; but instead of knocking the colours on, you must have a little more in your brushes and sprinkle or throw them on by a peculiar motion of the hand which you can only acquire by practice. First, red; next, black; thirdly, yellow; fourthly, blue; and lastly, with a larger brush and fuller of colour, you throw on the brown or predominating colour, beginning at the left-hand corner of the trough farthest from you, and working down and up closely and regularly all over, taking care not to go twice over the same place, or you will produce an appearance like rings by the falling of one spot upon another, which is objectionable. You must next take up the sheet of paper by the two opposite corners, and holding it by as small a portion as possible between the thumb and forefinger of each hand, keeping it nearly upright but inclining towards the left, you allow the corner held by the right hand gently to touch the floating colour, while, as soon as it touches, you must shake, agitate, or move it to and fro with a regular motion, at the same time gradually lowering the sheet of paper with the left hand till it is lying flat on the surface of the solution in the trough. On taking it up you will find it shaded in stripes, and where properly done it will have a very pretty and striking appearance, but of course it will require considerable practice to make it perfect. The brown colour will require to be much stronger in gall, as well as thicker in consistency than the vein colours; *a, b, c, d, e,* represent the colours as they appear in succession as thrown on. No. 3 *a* the same when shaded, as *f*, whether green, brown, or any other colour.

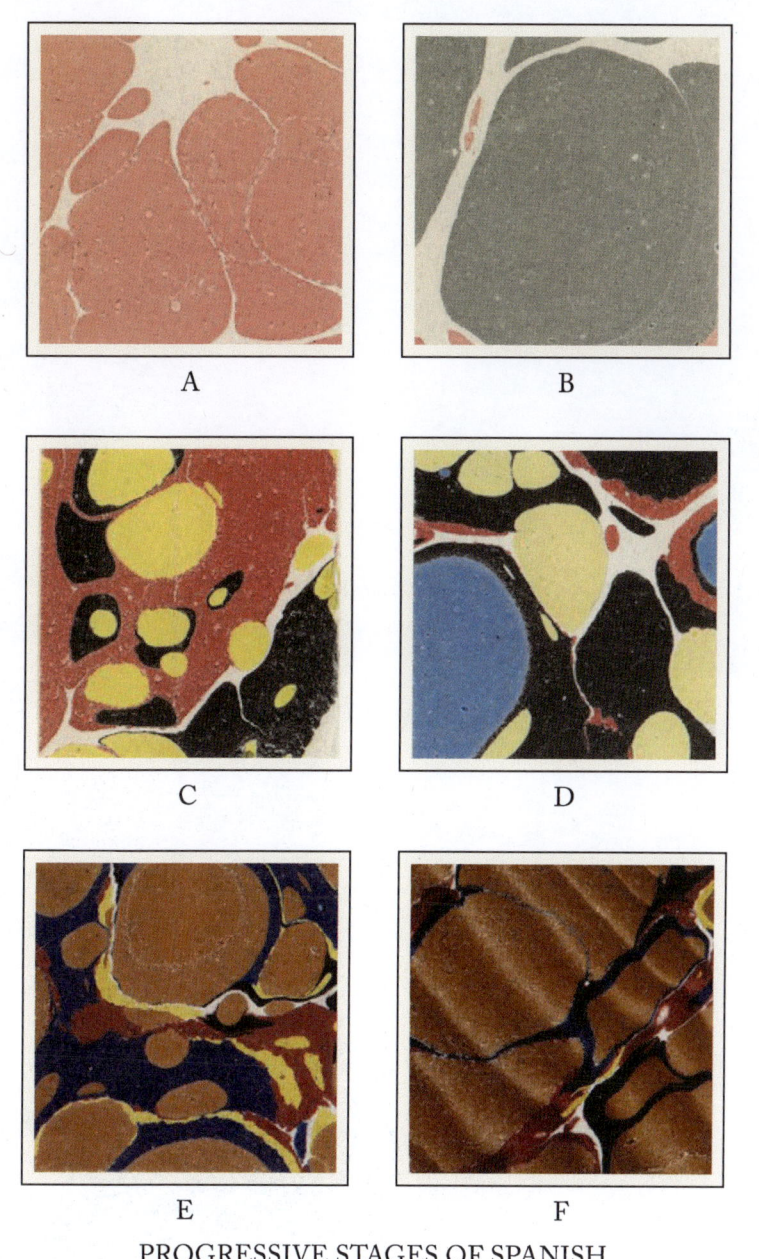

Example No. 4 — Fancy Spanish or Lace Pattern

EXAMPLE NO. 4

Fancy Spanish or Lace Pattern

This is rather a complicated and tedious pattern to make, but it has a very neat and pretty appearance when done well, and looks like a combination of the Italian with Spanish, which in fact to a great extent it is, the difference being this—that there are more colours in the veins, and the white is beaten on more finely, and the veins are not so closely driven up as in Italian itself, the last or principal colour being so tempered with gall as to drive the whole of the colours previously put on sufficiently close to produce the appearance of lace net between the spots lastly thrown on, which should be done rather liberally, so as to uniformly cover the whole; when this is done, lay on the paper in the same way as described in the previous pattern, shading it as it descends, and you will have the result shown in No. 4.

Example No. 5 — Spanish marble

EXAMPLE NO. 5

This is a pleasing variety caused by bending or folding the paper in squares or diamond shapes, producing somewhat the appearance of watered silk. There is no difference in the preparation of the colours required for this purpose, but it is more difficult to guide the paper in shading as you lay it down. A little more than half a century ago the so-called Spanish marble was unknown, and, like most novelties, commanded a very high price when it first came out; and various stories were circulated as to how it was first discovered, some of them ridiculous enough. One is as follows: A man was busily engaged on his work, and just as he was on the point of laying on his paper, another drove with some violence against his trough, by which the whole surface was agitated and set in motion like the waves of the sea, and the effect thereby produced excited further attention and study, ultimately resulting in the production of this very pretty description of marbling. I have also been credibly informed that the first that was made was done in the following manner:—One man got under the trough, and when the colour had been all put on, and the paper held in readiness to be laid down, he shook the trough so as to produce an undulating surface, when the paper was immediately applied, producing a wave-like appearance: these shades, however, were so broad and irregular when compared with those which are done by the present method, besides occupying the time of two to do the work of one, that it fell into disuse as soon as the improved method was brought to light. There was also another story current, which was this—and I am sorry to say that there is a considerable probability of an approach to truthfulness in it. A workman who had been indulging too freely in potations of strong drink came to his occupation one morning with a trembling, shaking hand and unsteady nerves: he could not hold a joint still, and alas! had neither money nor credit to get a drop more (just to steady him); so to work he must go as he was. But when he came to lay the paper down, his poor palsied hand shook so much that he spoiled (as he admitted) every sheet he tried. Some of this attracted the notice of the master, to whom the cause was explained, and the light thus thrown on the subject gave rise to further investigation and improvement, till at last the perfect development was obtained, and it became exceedingly popular and brought in a very liberal remuneration. I do not vouch for the truth of either of these statements, I merely give them as I received them; but it is not at all necessary for the object of this work either to receive or reject them.[1]

Size or medium: gum tragacanth and flea-seed for all Spanish patterns.

1   CWW: Since writing the above, the author has obtained possession of a book printed in Madrid nearly a hundred years ago; it appears to have been bound at the same time and place, and is lined inside with a rude kind of Spanish marbled paper, the outsides of the book are also covered with the same; and as both the texture and appearance of the marbled paper appear to be the same as that on which the book is printed, it seems evident that Spain can claim the; precedence of England in the production of that variety, and that the various statements which have been made with reference to its method of discovery should be received with caution. The book is now in the author's possession.

EXAMPLE NO. 6[1]

Extra or Drag Spanish.

This is another variety, for which at one time there was a great demand, and which stands out quite distinct from any of the others. In order to accomplish this, you must have a trough twice the size of the paper you intend to marble, as, in order to produce the elongated form of the spots, you must, instead of shading, draw or drag the sheet of paper from one end of the trough to the other, letting it fall about an inch at a time, each inch, as it were, overlapping the former, and adjusting your distances so as to let the last fall just as you arrive at the opposite side of the trough to the one from which you began. The colours and preparations may be just the same as for the other Spanish, only they must be considerably thinner, as from the circumstance that one sheet of paper being drawn over a surface usually allotted for two, the colours would accumulate so thickly on the paper that they would not only look muddy, but would also peel or scrape off, and not glaze. It is also more tedious to make, and of course more expensive than the ordinary kinds of Spanish, and always realizes a higher price.

---

1   See page 42.

Example No. 6 — Extra or Drag Spanish

EXAMPLE NO. 7

Nonpareil.

Perhaps no pattern that ever was produced has had such an extensive and prolonged run as this, and although it has now become so common as to be used on almost every description of work, it still holds its place in the favour of the public. About forty-five years ago it was sold at the extraordinary price of six shillings per quire for demy size, and that was very inferior to what may now be obtained for half-a-crown or three shillings.

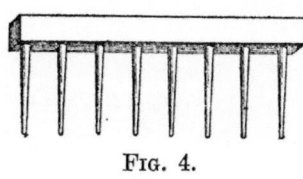

Fig. 4.

In order to do this description of marbling you must have a solution of gum tragacanth alone in the trough to work upon, and the colours, though mixed with gall and water, must be used thicker, and in larger quantities than for Spanish. The accompanying example will greatly help to facilitate your comprehension of the idea of the progress of the pattern through its various stages till completed. You must first begin by sprinkling the surface all over with red (a); secondly, black, see (b); thirdly, orange chrome, see (c); fourthly, blue, see (d); and lastly, buff, see (e). You must now take the peg-rake, which must be as long as the trough from right to left; this you must pass carefully and steadily up the trough from front to back through the colours, and down again from back to front, taking particular care when you draw it back that you bring the teeth of the rake exactly between the lines where they went up, and which, if left so, would produce a pattern in itself: see (f). Next, take your comb, which should be kept conveniently close to the trough in a narrow box filled with water, and gently draw it through the colour as formed by the rake from left to right, and the process is complete, ready for the laying-on of the paper, which should be done as quickly as possible. The result is shown in the example No. 7.

There may be many varieties made of this kind, both as regards the sizes of the combs, and the colours used for the various sorts of binding and books; for instance, a brown Nonpareil, and a black and brown combined, have been largely patronized for works of divinity; a red Nonpareil for military, and a green for floral; but they are all produced on the same principle and by the same kind of process as the first described, whether the colours employed be few or many: see example No. 8 on page 48.

Example No. 7. Part i. [Nonpareil pattern]

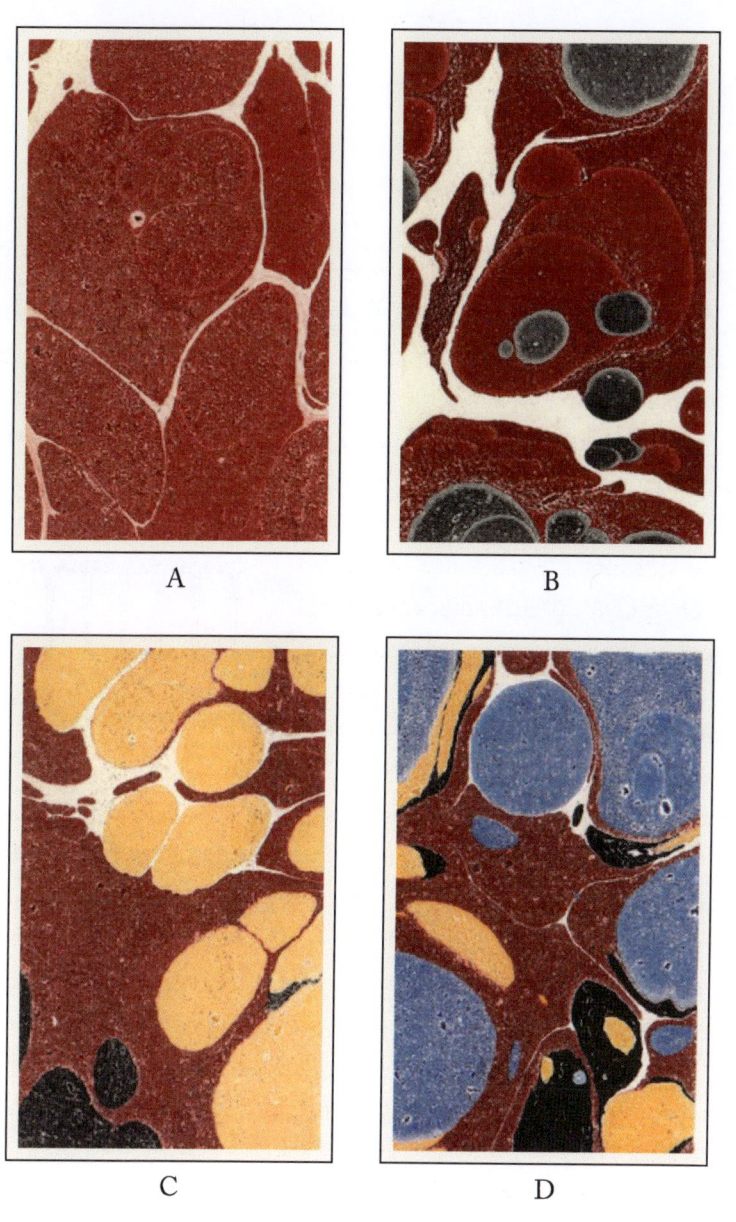

A

B

C

D

PROGRESSIVE STAGES OF NONPARIEL. PART I.

Example No. 7. Part II.

E

F

G

PROGRESSIVE STAGES OF NONPARIEL. PART II.

EXAMPLE NOS. 8, 9, 10

Curl

The colours for this pattern will require to be mixed and prepared in precisely the same way as the preceding or Nonpareil pattern; the size or medium, also the same—viz., gum tragacanth alone. Proceed as follows:—First, sprinkle on a fair body of red; secondly, blue; thirdly, green; and fourthly and lastly, yellow or orange, whichever you may prefer. You must next make your curls—as it would be very tedious to make these one by one—over as large a surface as a sheet of paper; and, as there would be considerable difficulty to keep them uniform, you will require an instrument formed something like a harrow in miniature, consisting of small bars of wood placed parallel with each other at regular distances, each containing a number of pieces of wire about three inches in length, inserted at intervals corresponding with the number of curls you require on your sheet of paper. Presuming, therefore, that you have your colours all on ready, you take this instrument in both hands, and dropping it equidistant from all sides of the trough, give it two or three turns with a rotary movement, lift it immediately out, lay on the paper, and you will have the pattern represented in the example No. 9 on page 49. Example No. 10 on page 50 has wider space and two movements, one the reverse way of the other.

Example No. 8 — Nonpareil pattern

Example No. 9 – Curl pattern

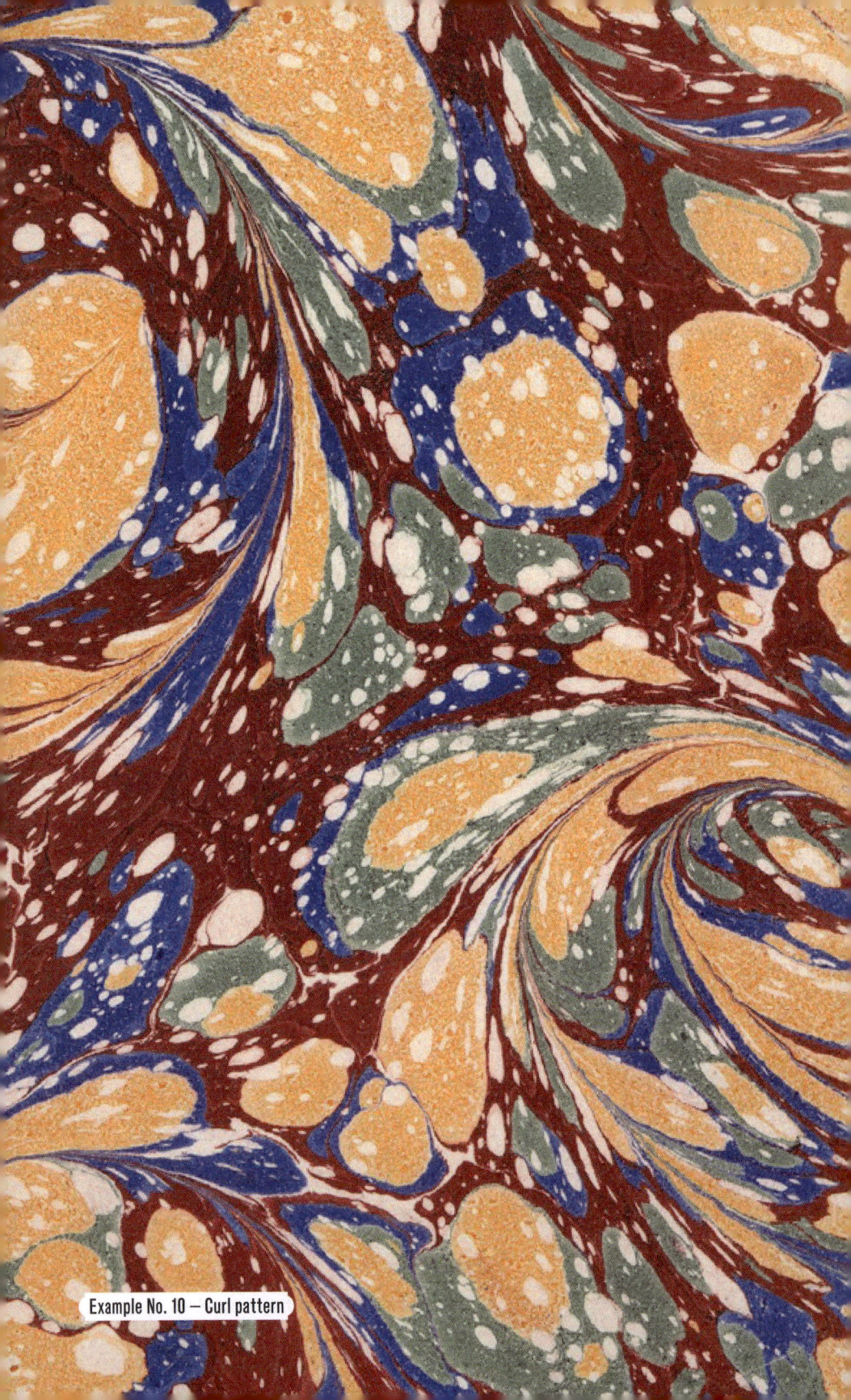

Example No. 10 – Curl pattern

EXAMPLES NOs. 11 AND 12

Zebra.

This is a very nice pattern when well made and requires to be kept clean. In working you must proceed in just the same manner as though you were going to make Nonpareil with the first four colours, viz., red, black, blue, and yellow or orange. When you have proceeded thus far you must rake it before you throw on the buff colour from front to back, and afterwards throw on the top or buff colour; lay on the paper flat for one pattern, and shade it as for Spanish for the other.

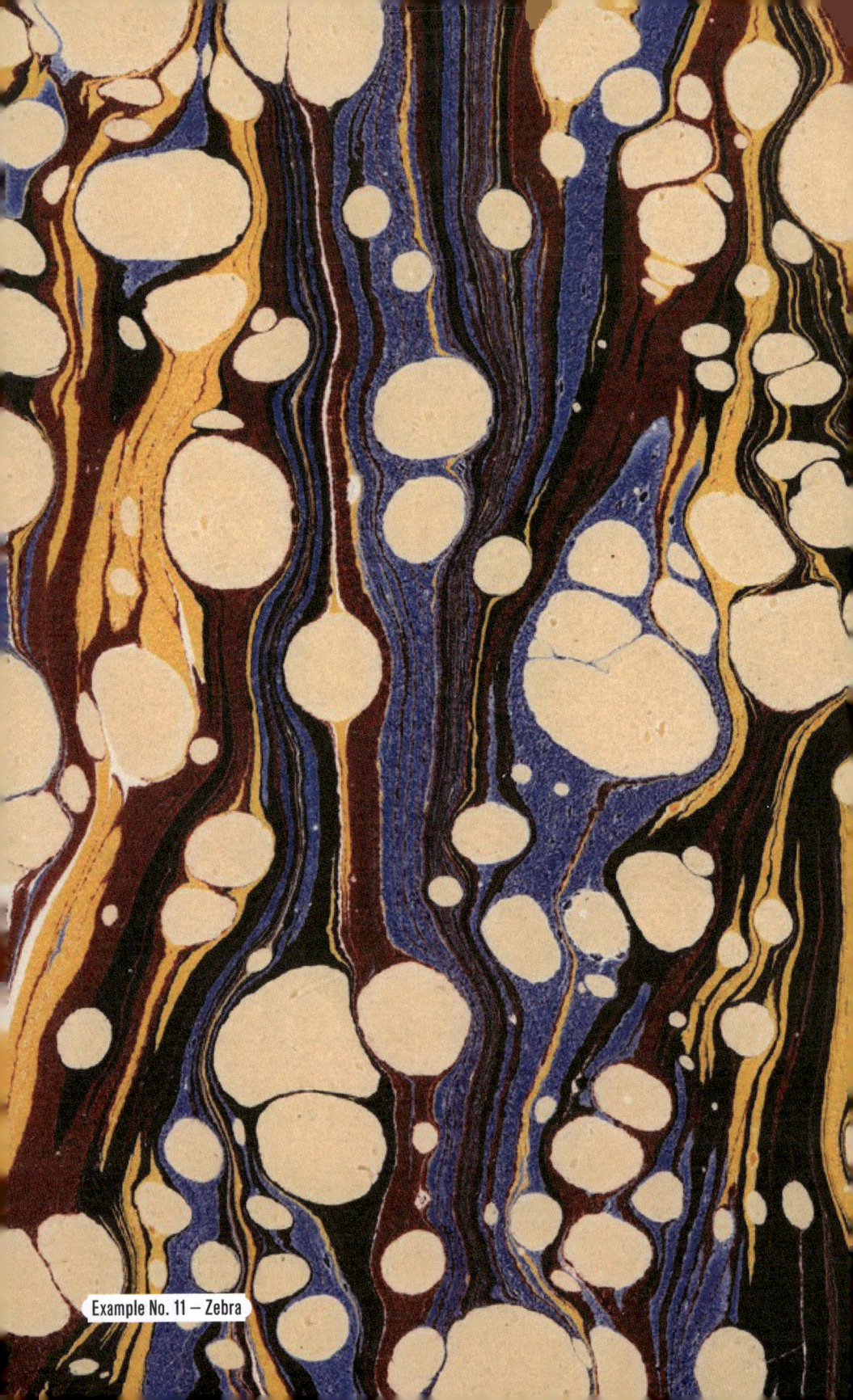

Example No. 11 – Zebra

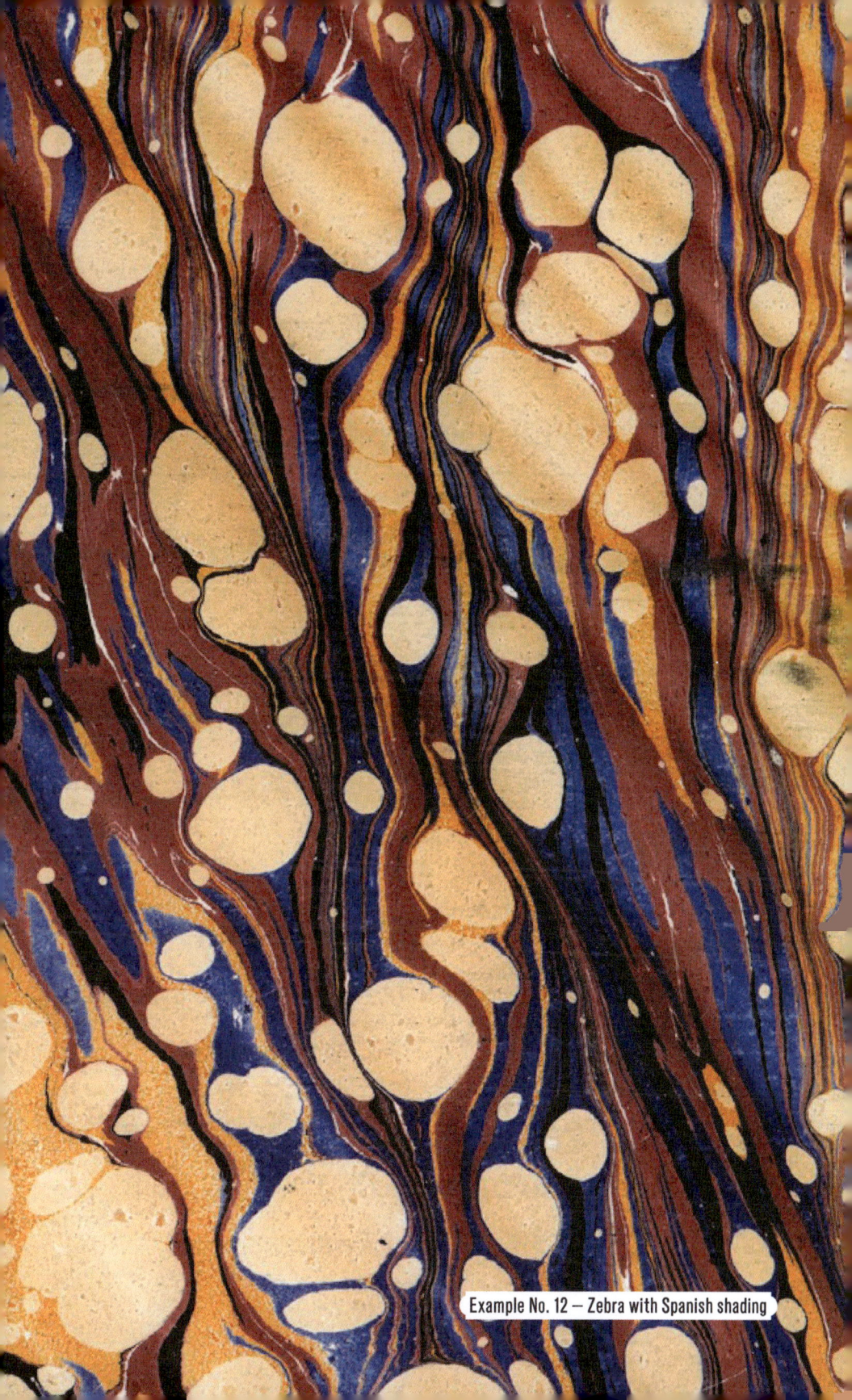

Example No. 12 — Zebra with Spanish shading

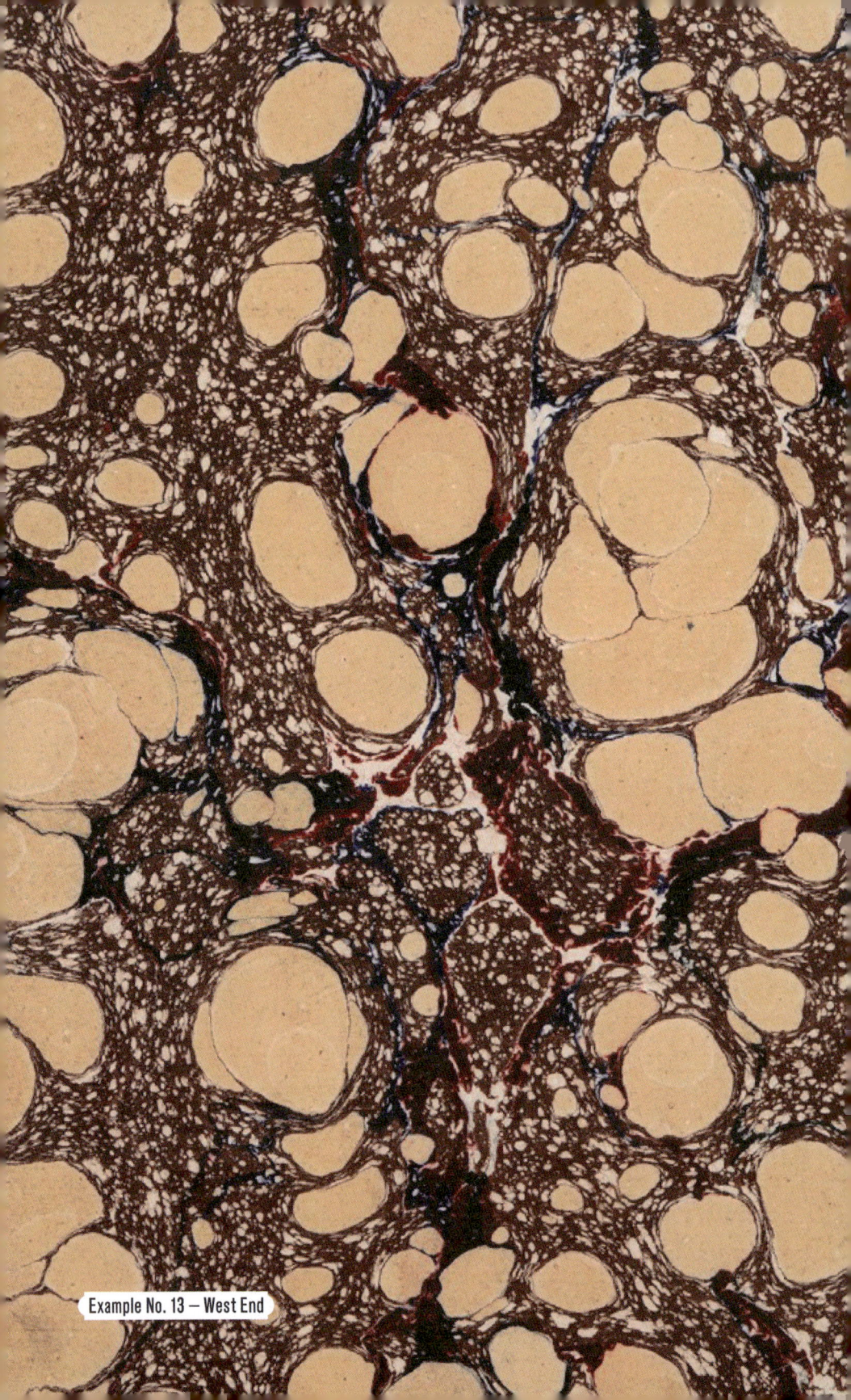

Example No. 13 — West End

EXAMPLE NO. 13

West End

This is a very neat, quiet pattern, and is in every respect similar to the Spanish in the working and throwing on of the colours, the principal difference being that the paper is laid down flat without being shaded. It consists of two prominent colours besides the veins: one of these is dark and dotted all over with small white spots, the other or top colour is light, and is made by taking a portion of the dark colour and adding to it and mixing up with it a quantity of white, sufficient to bring it to the required tint, and whether the predominant colour be brown, blue, or green, the same rule may be observed with all. Mix the vein colours with gall and water as in the instructions previously given for Spanish, then mix the dark brown thicker in body, and with a larger proportion of gall; sprinkle it on full, so as to drive the veins up fine; next take the white or gall and water, as in Italian, and beat or knock it on finely and evenly all over, but not so much as in the Italian; lastly, take the light or top colour which will require to be stronger in gall than any of the other colours, and sprinkle it lightly and evenly over all. Lay on the paper as quickly as possible, and the pattern is complete. The same preparation of gum and flea-seed will do for this as for the Spanish or Italian patterns.

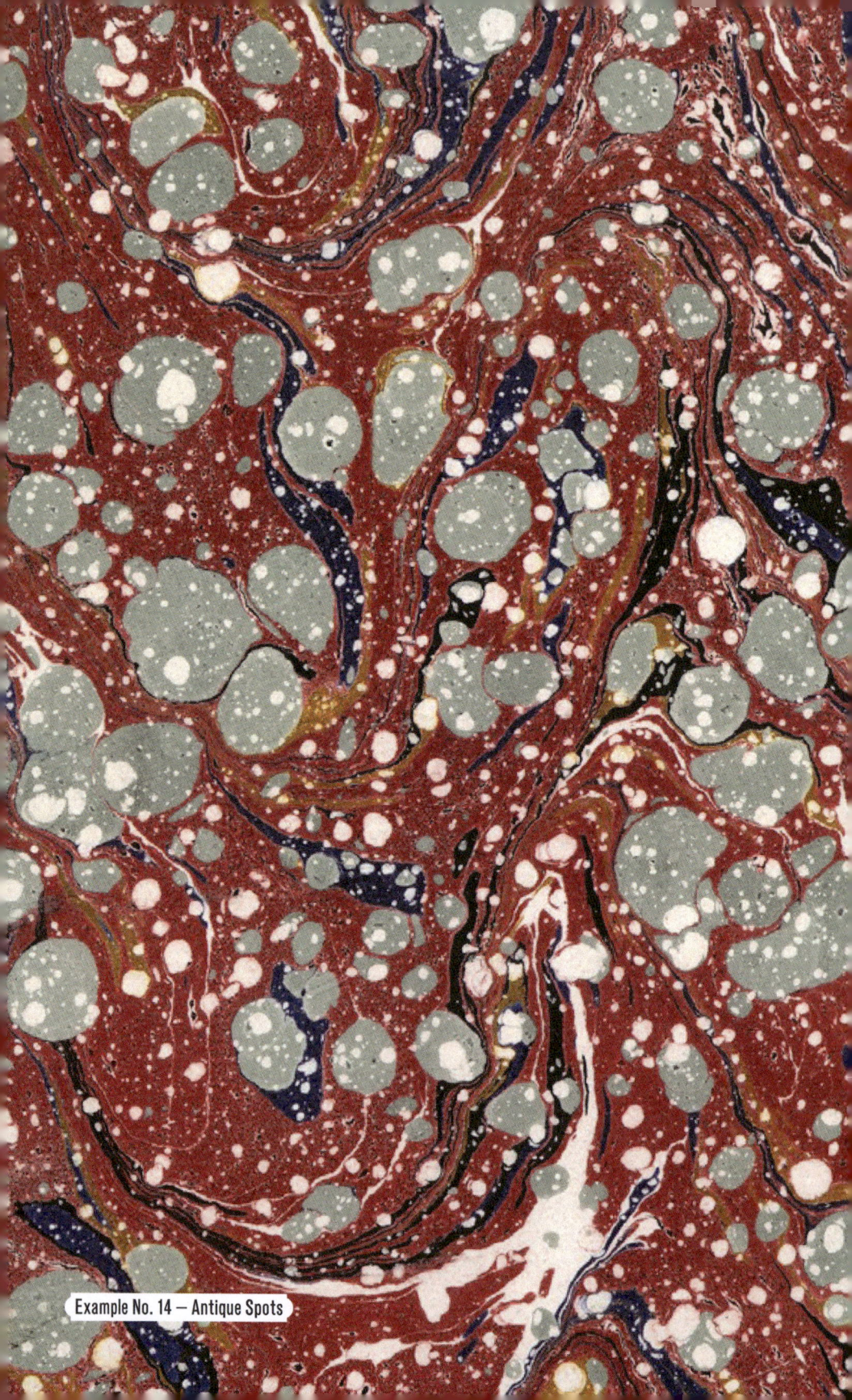

Example No. 14 — Antique Spots

EXAMPLES NOs. 14, 15

Antique Spots

There will now be no necessity for us to repeat or recapitulate the manner of mixing and throwing on the colours for the veins, etc., therefore useless repetitions will be avoided, as they will tend to confuse rather than to edify; however, any remarkable variations will still be specially noticed and duly impressed on the attention of the student. In this section of the art, you will find two examples, the colours being prepared the same as for Nonpareil and the same medium, viz., gum tragacanth, being used to work upon. When you have thrown on the three colours, red, black, and yellow, you must rake them as for Nonpareil before throwing on any more, after which proceed to throw on the other two; a little white to be beaten over the whole at last. The same rule to be observed whether the top colour be pink, blue, fawn, or any other shade. See Example No. 15.

Sometimes the raking is done as follows. A wider rake is used, with prongs of wire; this is taken through the first three colours from left to right, it is then again taken through with an up-and-down or undulating movement, after which the other colours are put on as described before. This gives a more elaborate appearance to the pattern, but we must leave everyone to their taste, as what one approves another may condemn. See Example No. 14 on page 56.

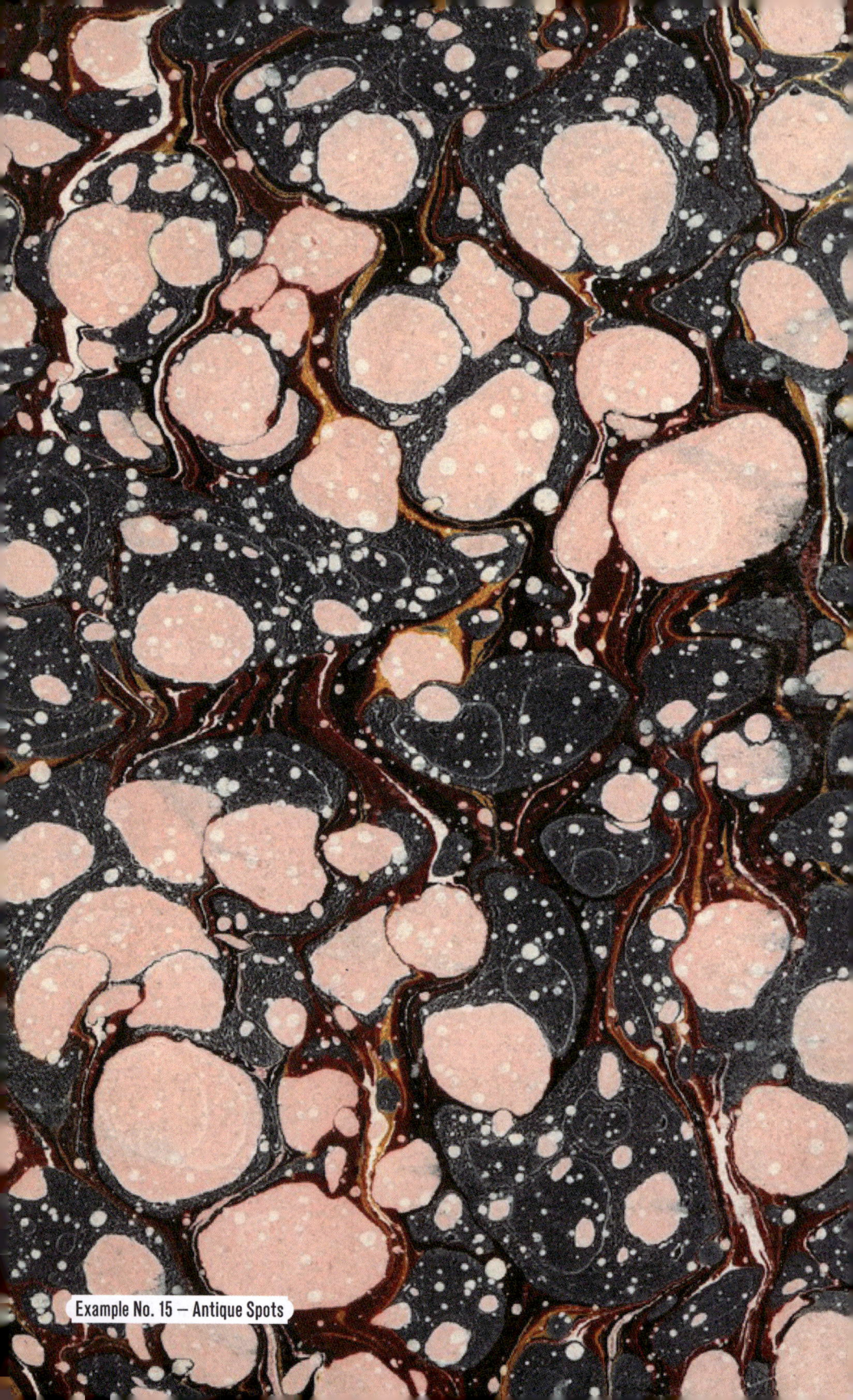

Example No. 15 — Antique Spots

EXAMPLES NOs. 16, 17

Antique, Straight, and Curled

The first stages of this pattern will have to be worked after the manner of Nonpareil, though the colours are; different, viz., first, red; second, yellow; thirdly, blue, and fourthly, green. You must now take your rake and after having drawn it through the colour from front to back and vice versa, you must beat a little white, not too freely, over it, and the pattern is completed. See No. 16 on page 60.

For the other (No. 17, page 61), in addition to the former, you either with a piece of wire, or a light frame with pieces of wire at certain distances, you must give a kind of curl one way and then shifting the frame so as to permit the points to come just between the spaces left untouched, give a gentle curve the reverse way, and again the pattern. is completed.

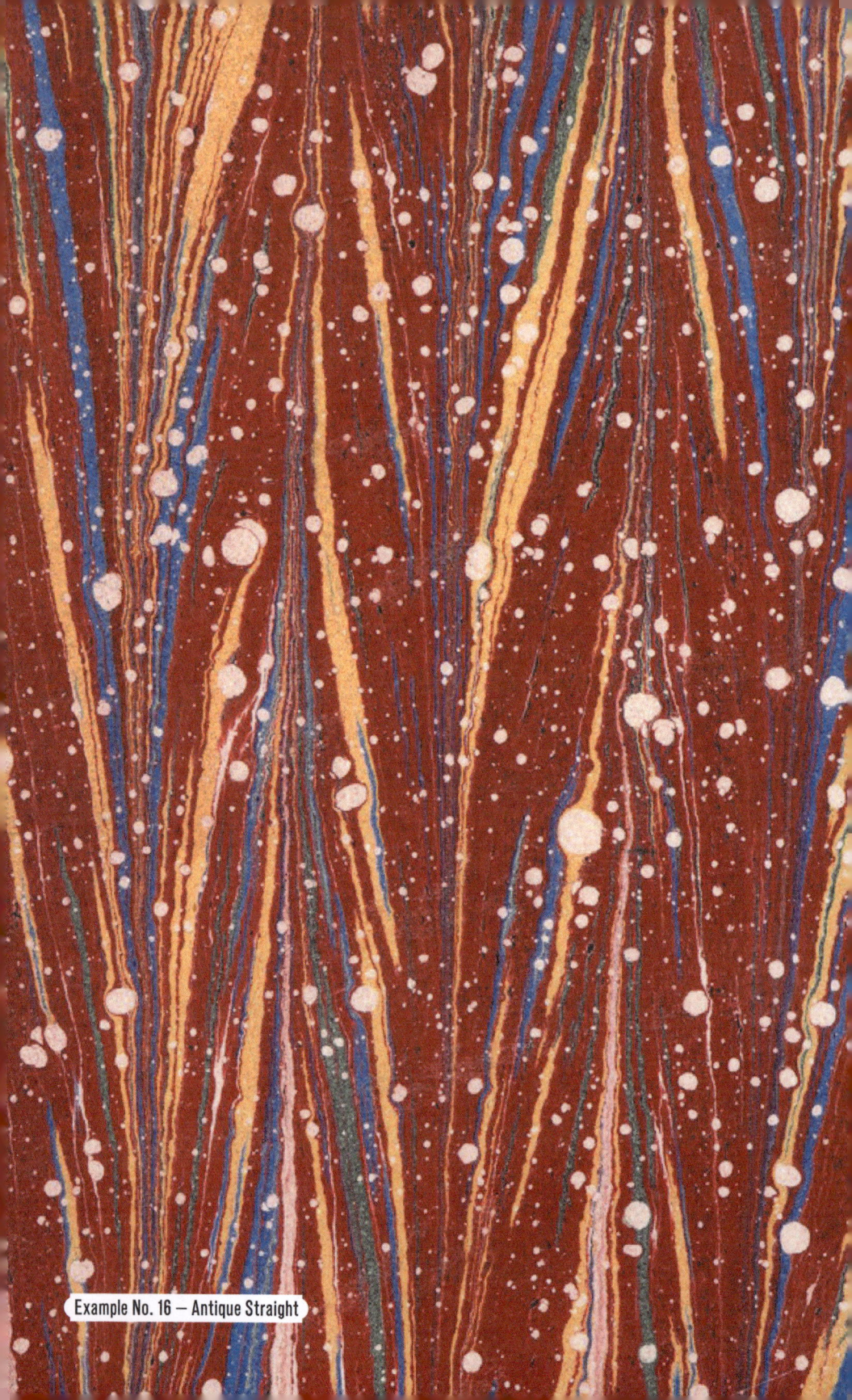
Example No. 16 — Antique Straight

Example No. 17 — Antique Curled

Example No. 18 — Antique Zigzag

EXAMPLES NOs. 18, 19

Antique Zigzag

Use colours same as for Italian, but rather thicker in consistence, and thrown on instead of beaten on, or if beaten on, fuller than for that. pattern; next beat on white, not too finely, then take an instrument which you may easily make yourself, as follows: Procure two pieces of wood about an inch square and two inches shorter than your trough from front to back; in these insert pieces of wire about two inches apart, more or less, according to the size of the wave you wish to produce; then fasten them: together so that the teeth or prongs of the one are exactly in the centre of the intervals of the other, the space between the two being regulated by a small piece of wood fixed between them, the thickness of which must be determined by the size of the pattern required. This you must move up and down as you draw it along through the colour from left to right, taking special care that the prong of the hind one just catches the bottom of the loop formed by the first, and you have the desired effect.[1]

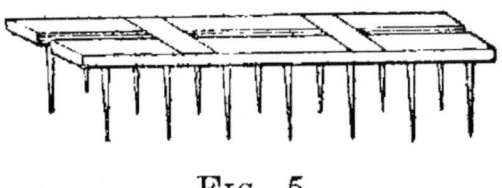

Fig. 5.

There are several variations of this style in use, both Shell and otherwise, indeed you may multiply patterns till you are confused.

---

1   This is commonly referred to as a double rake.

Example No. 19 — Antique Zigzag

EXAMPLES NOs. 20, 21, 22, 23

Old Dutch

This is one of the oldest and most esteemed patterns in use at this present period; it is more mechanical and requires a greater number of appliances than any of the previous sorts, and is accomplished by a very different process to any that have yet been noticed. If you take a sheet of this paper and examine it attentively, you will perceive that the colours are not scattered here and there in an indiscriminate confusion, but follow each other in regular succession diagonally across the whole sheet of paper, red being the preponderating colour.

In order to do this pattern well, your colours should be particularly well ground, and of the very best quality, they ought also to be mixed a day or two before using, that they may be as mellow as possible. If attention be not given to these instructions, your labour will be in vain, for you will never be able to produce satisfactory results, with either inferior or badly prepared materials.

You will require a number of small tins or pots, an inch and a half or two inches wide and about the same in depth—small jam pots will answer the purpose very well; you will also require two frames the size of the paper you intend to marble, in which are inserted a number of wooden pegs, about a quarter or three-eighths of an inch thick, fixed at regular distances about two and a half or three inches apart; both these frames must correspond exactly, and the pots of colour must be so arranged that the pegs will each drop into its respective pot of colour without any difficulty. It is with these you will have to put on the colours instead of brushes, with the exception of the red alone, which will have to be thrown on with a brush.

Y	B	Y	B	Y	B
G	Y	G	Y	G	Y
Y	B	Y	B	Y	B
G	Y	G	Y	G	Y
Y	B	Y	B	Y	B
G	Y	G	Y	G	Y

The colours required are red, blue, green, yellow, and white, and as you will not be able to mix these colours in the small pots, you must procure four large jugs with spouts, capable of holding about three pints of colour—a jug for each colour; in these the colours must be mixed, and be made all right for working before putting them into the little ones. In order to ascertain this you must try them by dipping into each a piece of stick and letting a drop fall on the solution (having first thrown on a little red), and tempering it with gall till it spreads out to the desired extent; when they are all right for working, you proceed to fill the little pots and arrange them in the order shown in the diagram, one lot of the pots being filled with nothing but white,[1] and the other lot numbering the same in quantity, filled, or rather half filled, with the three colours, green, blue, and yellow, denoted in the diagram by G, B, and T. When you have done this and arranged them conveniently as near the trough as possible without interfering one with the other, take the two frames of pegs and drop them carefully into the pots in such a manner as will enable you by a rotary motion of the frame with both hands to stir round the colour without upsetting the pots. You may now commence operations for the final procedure by first skimming the surface, then with a moderate-sized brush throw on a pretty good body of red, then lift carefully and gently your first frame, consisting of white only (always remembering first to

1   CWW: Instead of pots for the white, it will be less trouble to fill a trough with white, about an inch deep, in which you place the first frame of pegs, and as white costs little, you can afford a little waste.

give it a slight rotary movement so as to keep the colour from settling at the bottom of the pot, which it will very soon do)—gently, I repeat, lest you should shake the drops of colour off before you get it to its proper place over the red, and just let the tip of each peg touch the surface of the floating red all parts at the same time; quickly lift it off, placing it again in the pots ready for the next time, then quickly and carefully take the other with the three colours and let the points deposit a single drop of colour as exactly as you can in the centre of the drops of white just put on. You must now take a tapering stick—a stout brush-handle is as good a thing as any—and pass it up and down through the colours as they are now arranged on the trough from front to back at regular distances till you have gone over the whole extent of the surface, then pass your comb through from left to right, and you have Old Dutch, large or small, according as your comb may be; when you have lifted the paper out as it hangs on the stick, pour gently a little clean water over it, as that will wash away all the superfluous colour and gum and make it look clear and bright, which it will not do unless you wash it; still, even this will require to be performed with judgment, or you may wash off or impoverish the colours instead of improving them. It may also be done by putting on the three colours first, and the white after, the colours being adjusted accordingly.

When curls are required, of course you must have another frame with wires, according to the number and size of the curls required.

Some patterns are made by drawing through a second and larger comb, and sometimes even a third, but the more the colours are worked or drawn about after they are floated on the solution, the more likely they are to get broken and deteriorated in appearance to the eye.

Some use a rake similar to that spoken of for Nonpareil, but for this pattern the brush-handle is preferable.

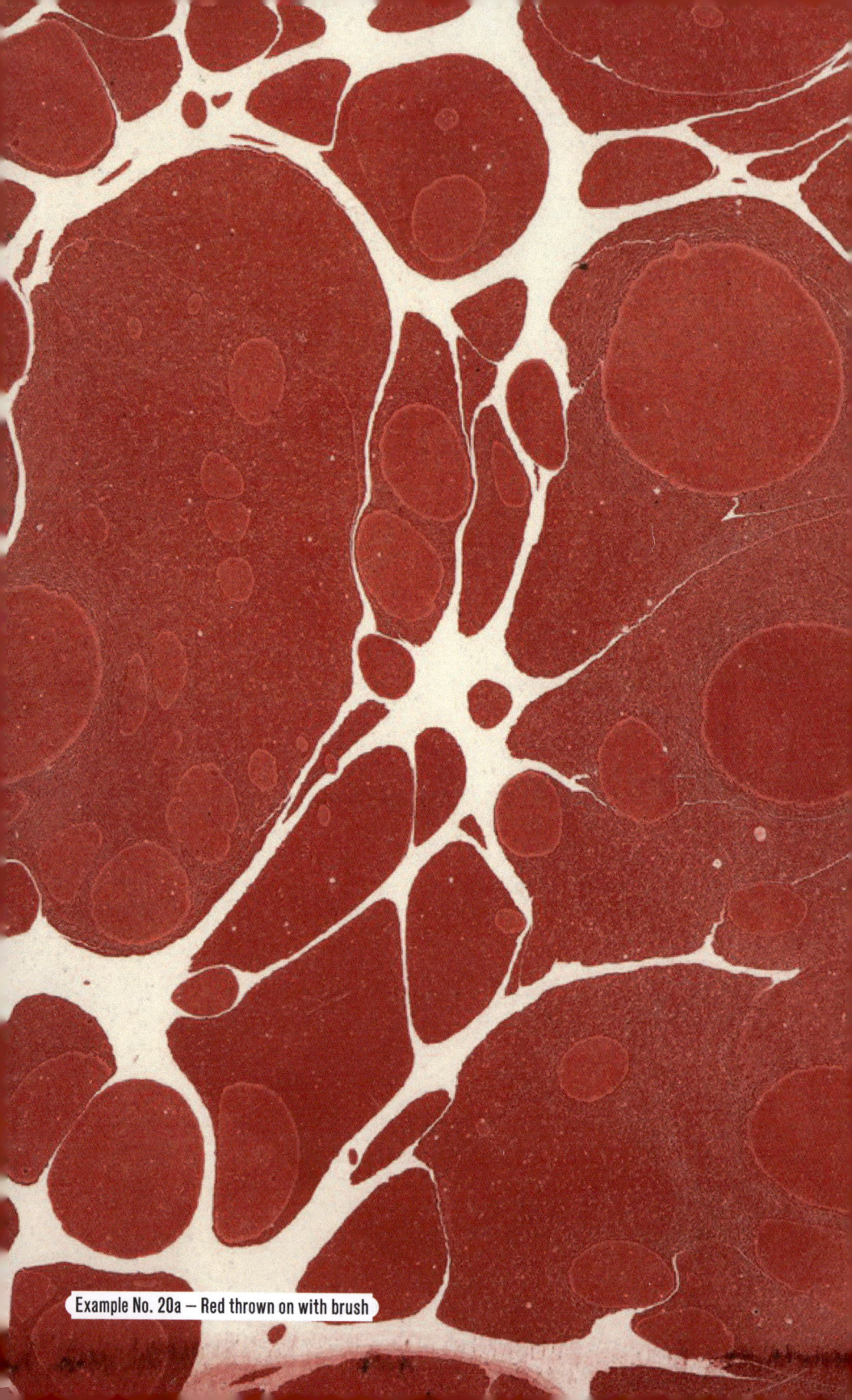
Example No. 20a — Red thrown on with brush

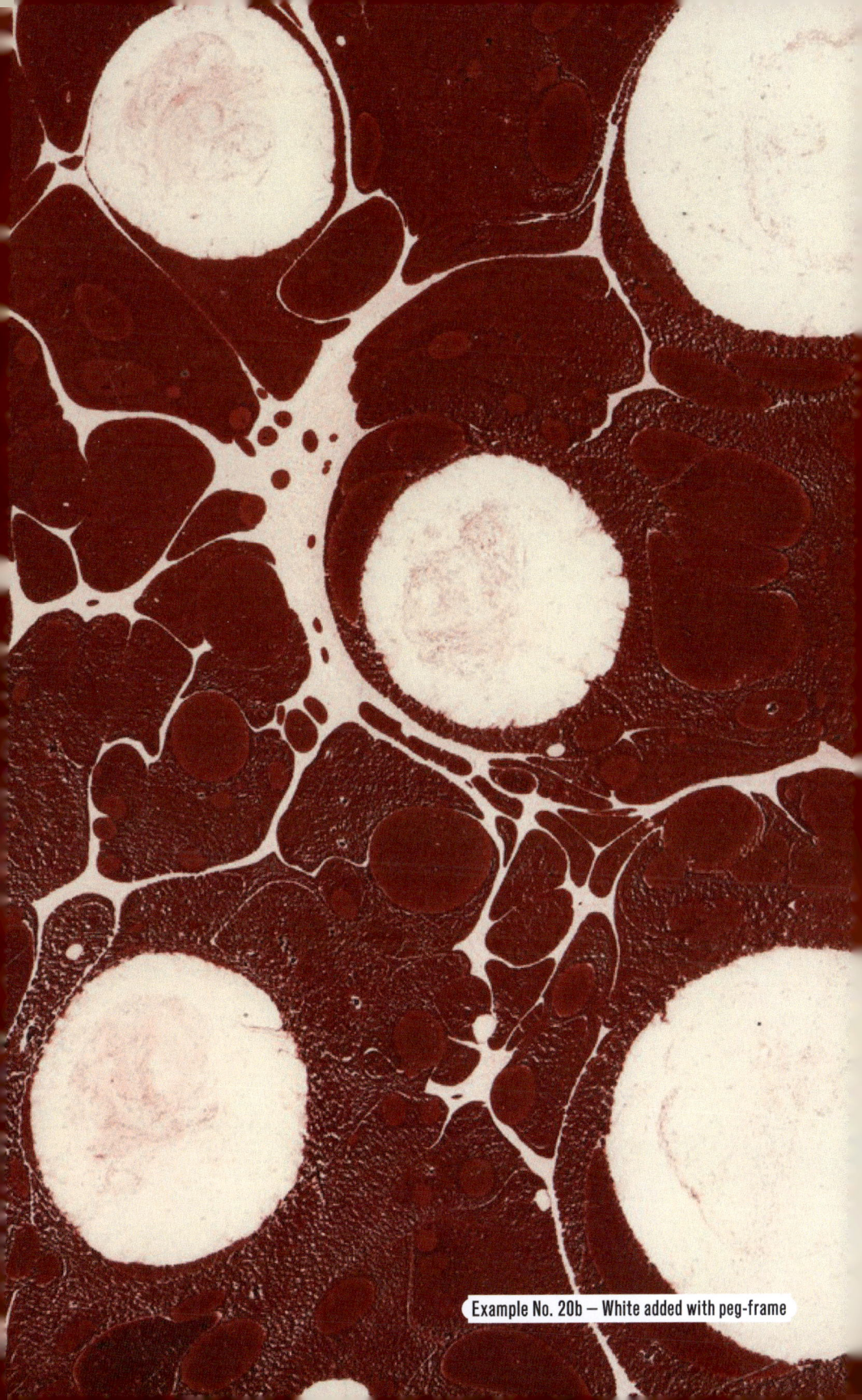

Example No. 20b — White added with peg-frame

Example No. 20c – Colors added with peg-frame

Example No. 20d — Drawn up and down with brush handle

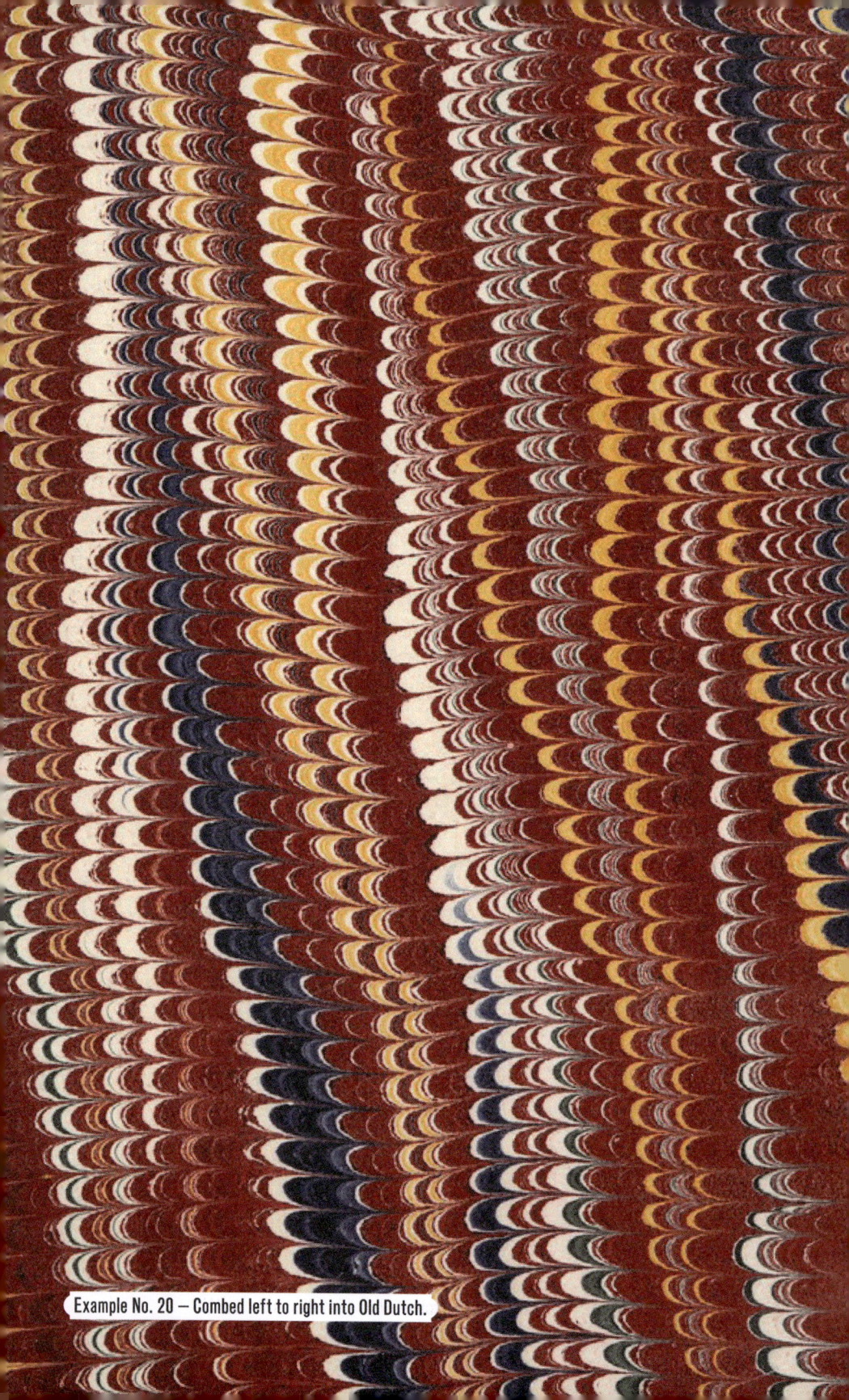
Example No. 20 — Combed left to right into Old Dutch.

Example No. 21 — Old Dutch with curls made with wire frame

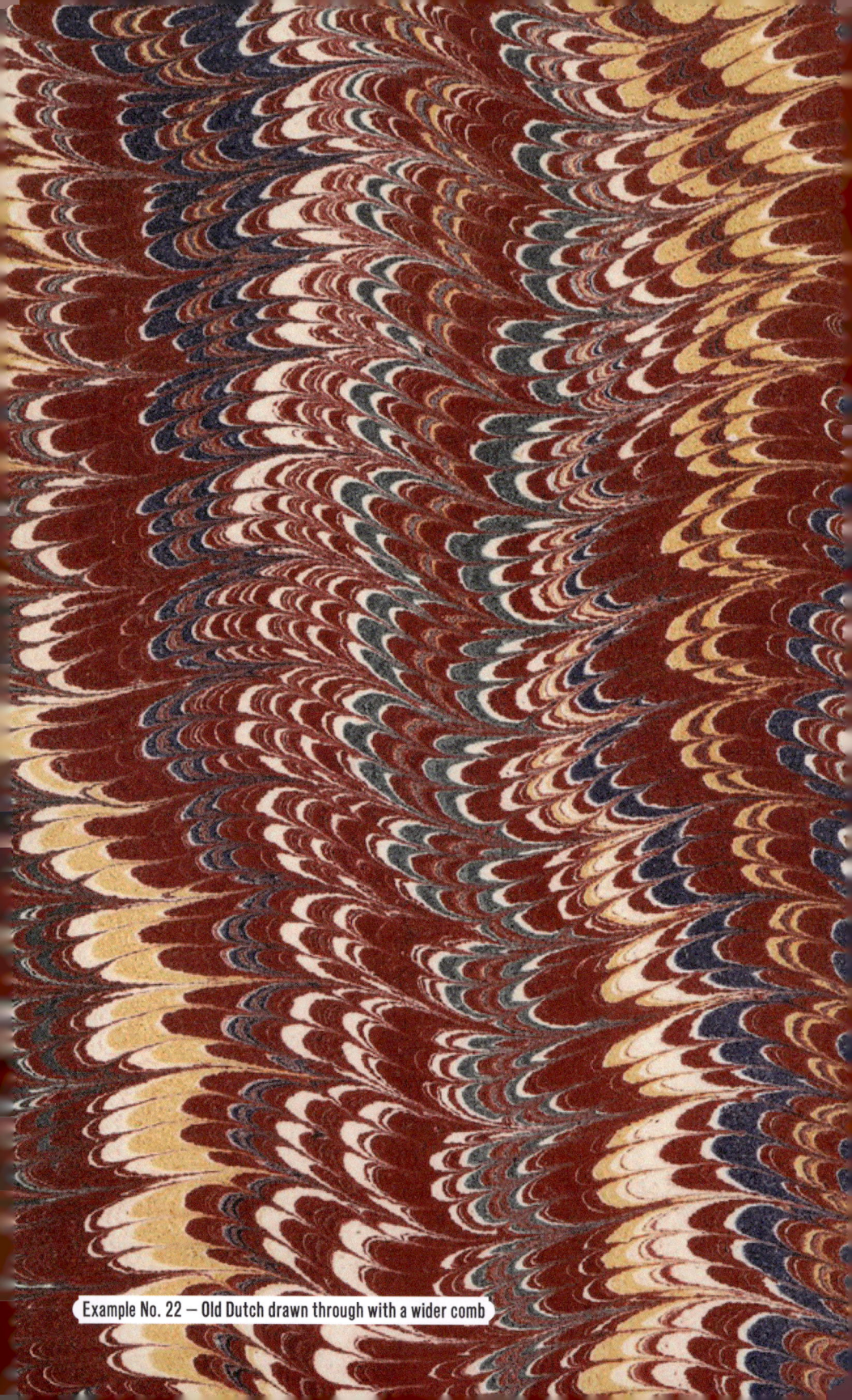

Example No. 22 — Old Dutch drawn through with a wider comb

Example No. 23 — Large Old Dutch

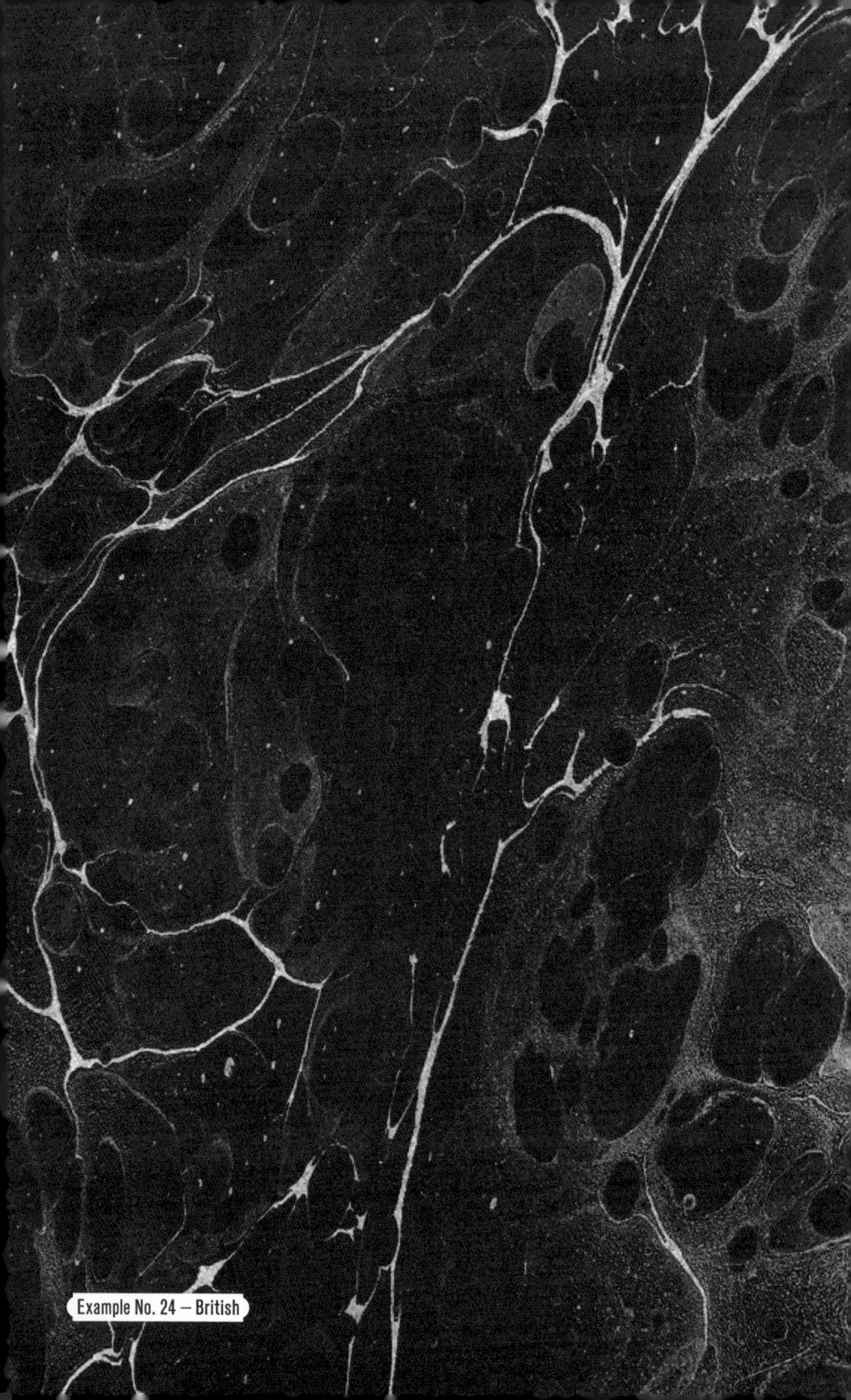
Example No. 24 — British

EXAMPLE NO. 24

British

This is not a very easy pattern to execute, although it has so unpretending and simple an appearance, as it requires a good deal of practice and judgment to keep up any degree of uniformity. Some of the patterns are made with and some without veins. It must be done in a trough double the length of the paper you use, as it must be dragged or pushed from one end of the trough to the other in the same manner as directed for the Drag or Extra Spanish, and the size or solution must be the same, viz., a mixture of flea-seed and gum tragacanth.

Proceed as follows:—Take two jars and a large plate or dish, mix your colour, whatever it may be, in one of these jars in the same way as you would for ordinary Spanish, pour some of it into the other jar, and dilute it with a considerable portion of gall and water so as to make it much thinner in consistency, but more powerful in its spreading or flowing-out propensities, pour on the plate about a dessert-spoonful of the last or thin colour, and then, taking the brush out of the thicker colour, press it down on the other colour on the plate rather hardly, at the same time just giving it a twist round so as partially to amalgamate the two without combining them too closely. Proceed immediately to sprinkle on all over the trough; the light and dark spots will fall together, intermingling with each other, and producing that variegated and motley appearance which characterizes the pattern. In laying on the paper, you must draw it in the same manner as for the Drag Spanish; black alone used in this way on a coloured paper has a very unique appearance, and is, in fact, more like marble of some kinds than much of what bears the name of marble paper.

Thus far we have gone without the aid of any other acting agencies than gall and water alone; if such results as these can be produced with such simple materials, may we not be justified in expecting at some not very remote period far greater and more surprising effects from the advancement of scientific and chemical research, and its application to things hitherto considered by the many as beneath their notice, but which nevertheless involve mysteries which, with all their attainments, they are unable to solve, and so pooh-pooh them as commonplace and undignified withal.

EXAMPLES NOs. 25, 26, 27, 28, 28A, 29

French or Shell Marble

The colours for this kind or variety may be prepared very nearly in the same way as for the Spanish or West End, but the vein colours may be a little thinner, and the top or principal colour not quite so strong in gall, but in addition to the gall a few drops of oil may be mixed and well stirred up in it: put in but a few drops at a time, stirring it well with the brush every time you add to it, trying it occasionally till it produces the desired effect, which should be the appearance of shell-like rings, darker in the centre than round the edges. Be very careful in mixing in the oil, as too little will make it full of unsightly holes, while too much will cause it to lose the shell or ringy appearance altogether, and to spread out in such a manner as to destroy the appearance of the pattern entirely; there will be no way of rectifying this but by mixing some more colour without any oil, and adding it to that which contains too much.

We will, as at the beginning, commence with a single colour, without any vein, and a very neat pattern may be produced therewith, and called Small Blue Shell. The blue may be made with a mixture of indigo, rose pink, and Chinese blue, or damp Chinese blue where it can be procured; you must also provide yourself with a small iron rod or bar about 12 or 14 inches long, not too heavy. This you must place on your left hand, so as to be conveniently taken up when you require to make use of it, which in the small patterns will be with every colour you use, as well with the vein as the body colours; but in this instance, having but one colour and no veins, you will have but little difficulty in accomplishing your task. Presuming, therefore, that you have your colour right, and everything in order, you, as usual, steadily skim the solution or mixture in the trough, and with a tolerably good brushfull of the colour in your right hand and the rod in your left, you proceed to beat or knock the stock of the brush against the rod; go equally and uniformly all over, taking care that the colour falls in spots as near to one uniform size as possible, otherwise it will have a cloudy and imperfect appearance. In order to accomplish this desirable object, you must hold the bar at least at an elevation as high as your head, which will cause the spots to extend over a greater space, and to become finer as they descend, while if you hold it too low it will be a difficult matter to preserve uniformity. You must also be careful to keep the ring of the brush wiped from the superfluous colour which will accumulate upon it in the course of operation, and which will fall off in large spots or blotches, giving the work an most unsightly appearance.

You introduce three veins, red, yellow, and blue, mixed with gall and water, instead of knocking the brush against the iron bar, you must

Example No. 25 – Small Blue Shell

sprinkle them on with a peculiar shake of the hand only attainable by practice. The colour (brown), mixed in the same was as the preceding pattern, but sprinkled on evenly all over the red and yellow and blue, driving those three colours into veins, produces large Brown Shell or French, as No. 26. Brown is produced in the same way, but knocked or beaten on.

We will now contrast these with two well-known old patterns, called by the trade Large and small Fawn. The small is made with only a blue vein, the large with both black and blue. The colour called Fawn is pure Oxford ochre, burnt without any other colour mixed with it, and is mixed, in the same way as the blue in the previous example, with gall water and a little oil. These were very popular fifty years ago, and had a great run, the large Fawn for stationery work especially, but are now superseded by importations from the Continent, which have interfered with the manufacture of the commoner kinds of marbled papers in this country. (Nos. 27, 28.)

Sometimes two or more Shell colours are worked one over the other with good effect. One specimen of this description is introduced here, but as in former instances the last colour requires to be mixed with both more gall and oil to make it expand over the colour preceding it. (See example No. 28 a, page 85.)

Having thus far explained the principles contained in the production of the Shell or French marbles, we will introduce another variety in which the French and Spanish are combined, and sometimes with good effects. In order to do this, you must first produce on the solution a small French pattern, but with a considerably less amount of colour than you would put on for French alone, and for this reason, because it would require an amazing strength of gall to make the Spanish colour flow out over a complete Shell pattern, and if it did so flow out it would so close up the Shell that it would have a most muddy and confused appearance; therefore you must not have your French or Shell mixture so strong as for Shell itself, and your top or Spanish colour will then flow pleasantly over it with good effect, and produce a very pretty variety, whatever colours you may fancy to make it with. It is sometimes called Spanish with Shell veins. (See example No. 29, page 86.)

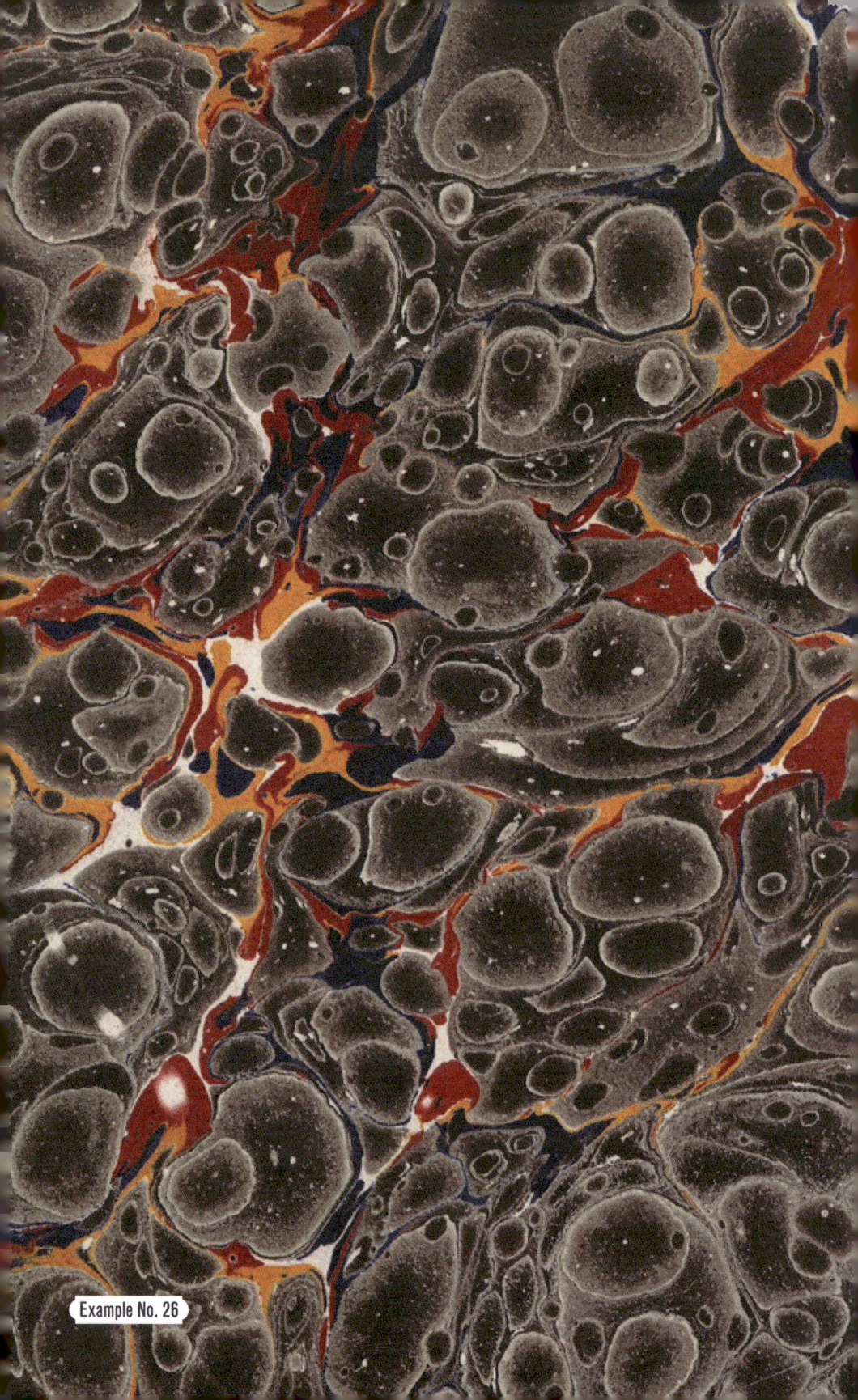

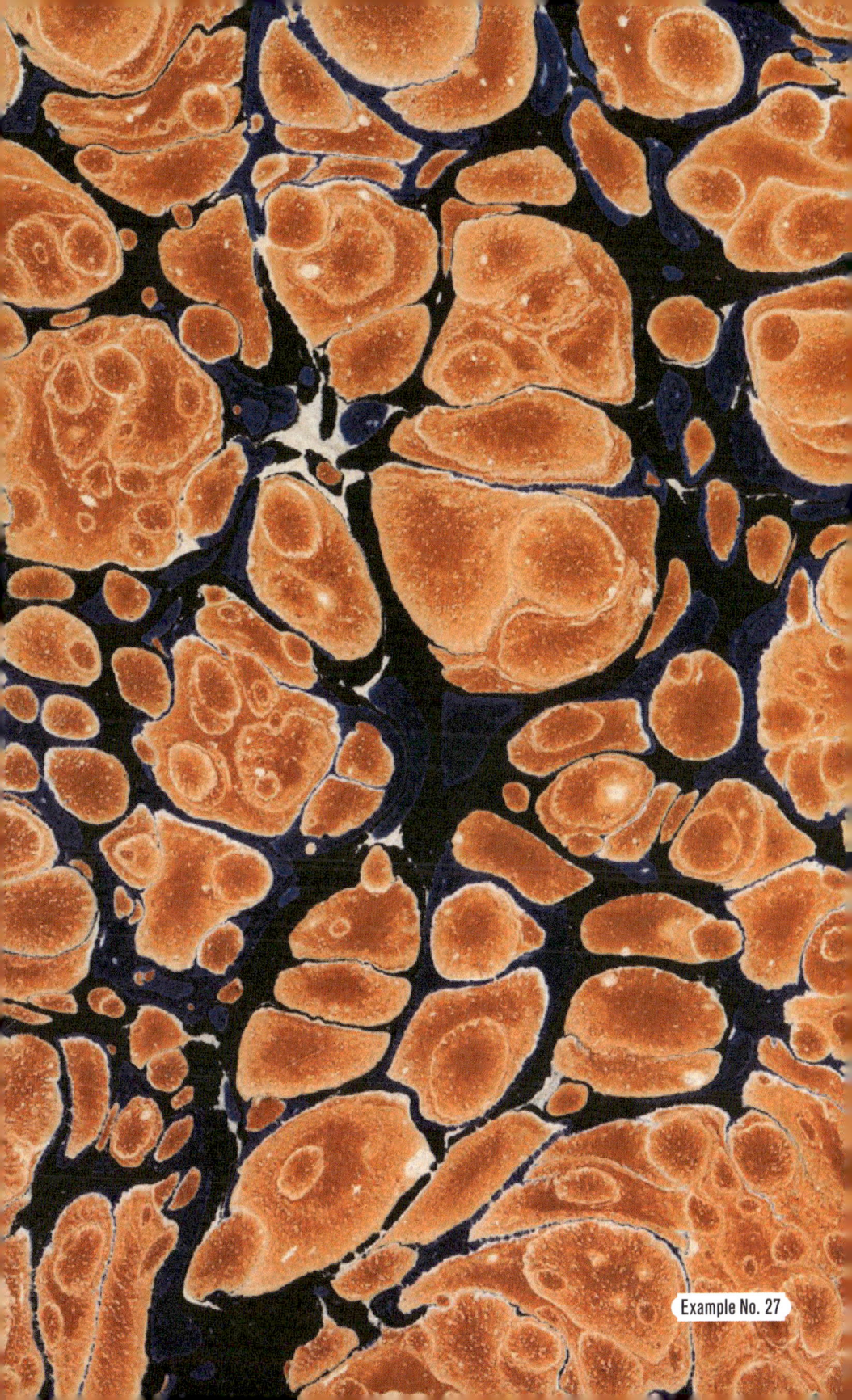
Example No. 27

Example No. 28

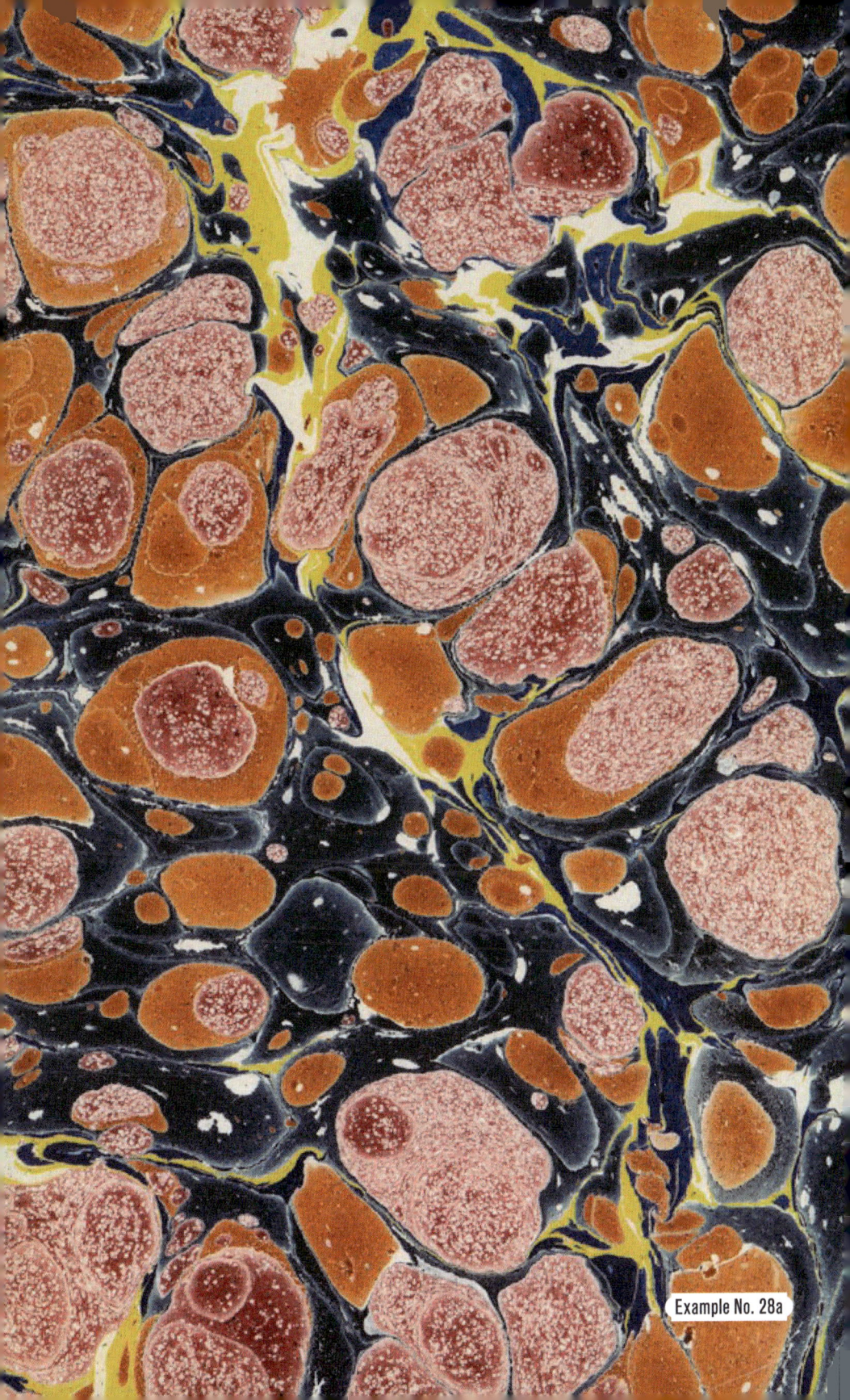
Example No. 28a

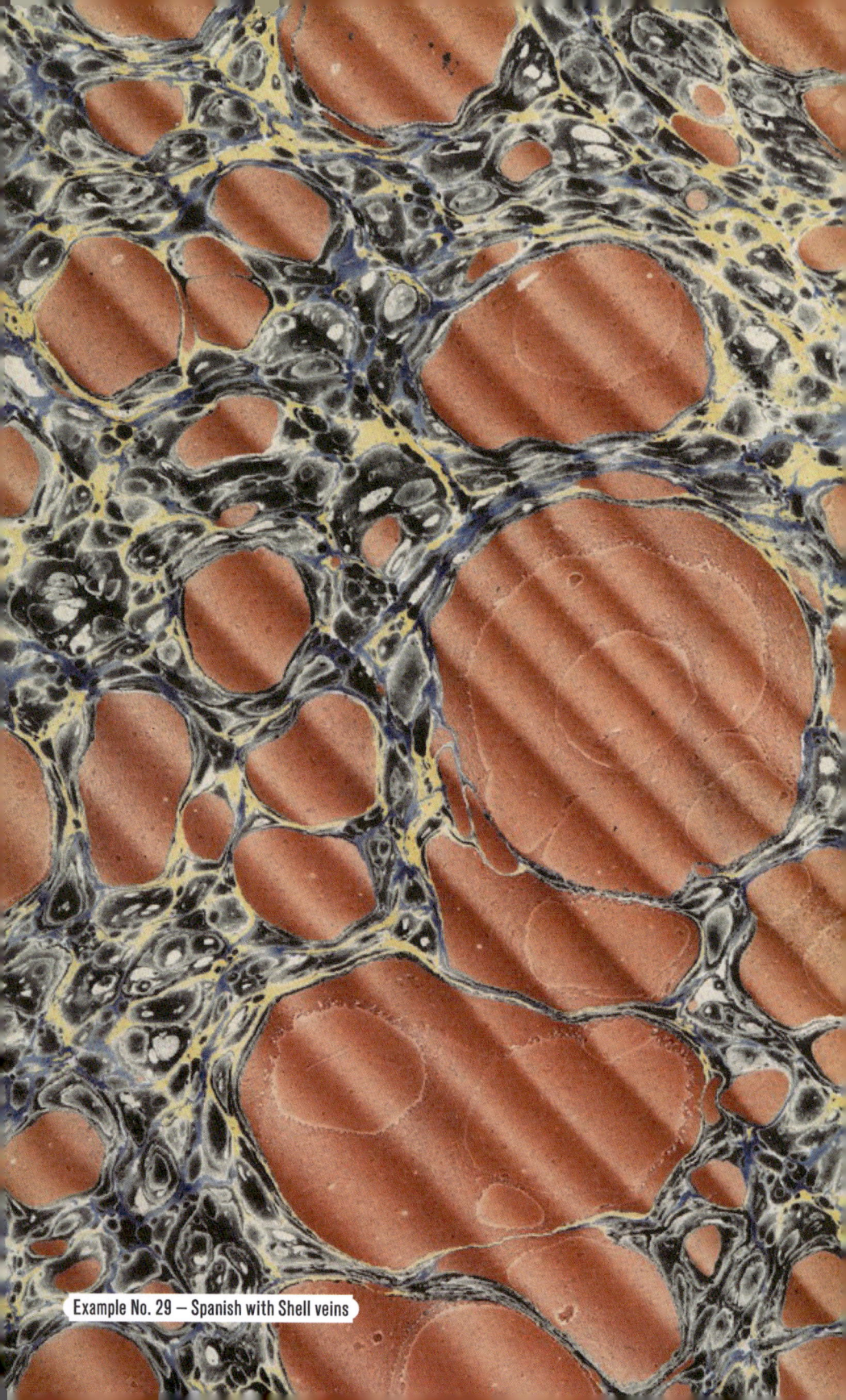
Example No. 29 — Spanish with Shell veins

EXAMPLE NO. 30

Stormont

We will now introduce another ingredient to the notice of our students, and that will be spirits of turpentine; its effect, when properly mixed and incorporated with the colour, is to cause it to break into fine holes like a network when it falls on the solution in the trough. It is used principally in the production of one of the oldest patterns extant, bearing the name of Blue Stormont, and though apparently a very simple pattern, consisting of only two colours, it is nevertheless one of the most difficult to keep in working order, owing chiefly to the very speedy evaporation of the spirits of turpentine, and the chemical action which is always going on among the ingredients with which the colour is mixed up; and it requires acute observation and great quickness of manipulation on the part of the operator to keep it anything like uniform in appearance.

The same mixture or preparation of gum and flea-seed will do for this as for the Spanish or French. The colours to be used will be red and indigo; no other blue will answer the purpose. Good indigo alone, and well ground—without which you will not be able to produce the proper effect—must be employed, and mixed with gall water and spirits of turpentine, of which the last ingredient a considerable proportion must be used. You must keep it constantly stirred, especially when your red vein is thrown on and you are ready for the other, taking the brush between both hands and twirling it backwards and forwards through the colour in the jar; and you may do this without fear of frothing it, as the spirits of turpentine will prevent that, and when you sprinkle it on the solution it will immediately fly out, and then as speedily contract or close up again, and appear to be in constant motion as it floats upon the surface, driving up the red, which of course is mixed with gall and water, as all the vein colours should be, into a fine vein, which relieves what would otherwise be a monotonous appearance. As before remarked, it is a very extraordinary pattern to manage. Sometimes it will go well at the very first trial, or at other times you may waste hours and not succeed to your satisfaction, but after letting the colour stand for a day or so it will work well, and give you no further trouble.

Should the holes in the pattern come too large, it may be from either an excess of the spirits of turpentine or from too little—nothing but experience will enlighten you on this point. If, however, it should be from too much, add a little more gall with a little more indigo, with a few drops of alum-water, but you must be very careful of this, for if you put in too much it will make the colour thick and clotted, in which case you must have recourse to a little weak solution of pearlash; but it is best, if possible, to do without either of them, as the more ingredients you put in the more difficult you will find it to control their effects; but when you get it right, it is one of the quickest patterns ever made.

The Stormont, which name is applied to all colours which have turpentine in them, is also used in combination with French or Shell colours, sometimes being thrown on lastly over the Shell, at other times under the Shell, or the Shell colours last, both having a very good effect.

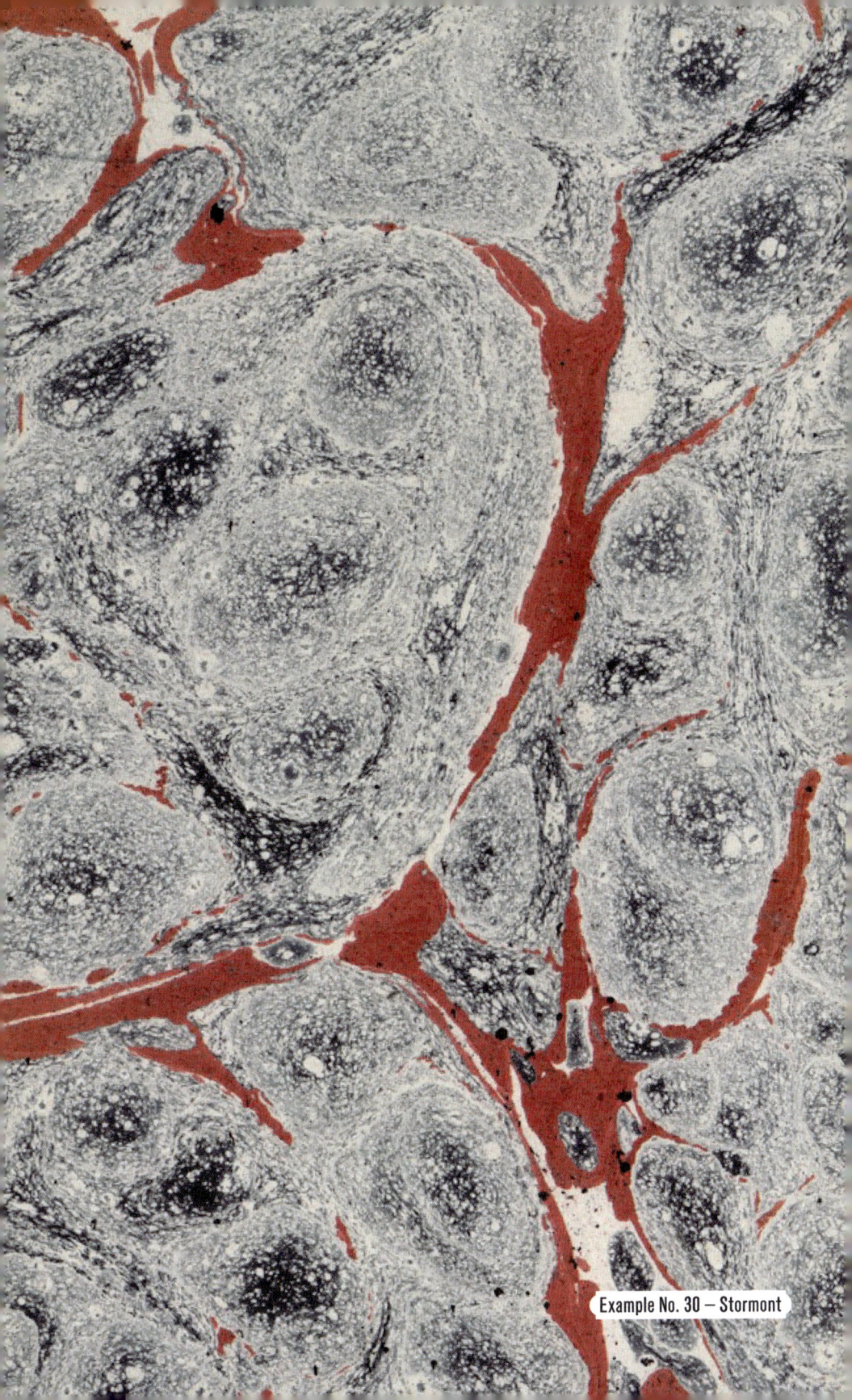

Example No. 30 — Stormont

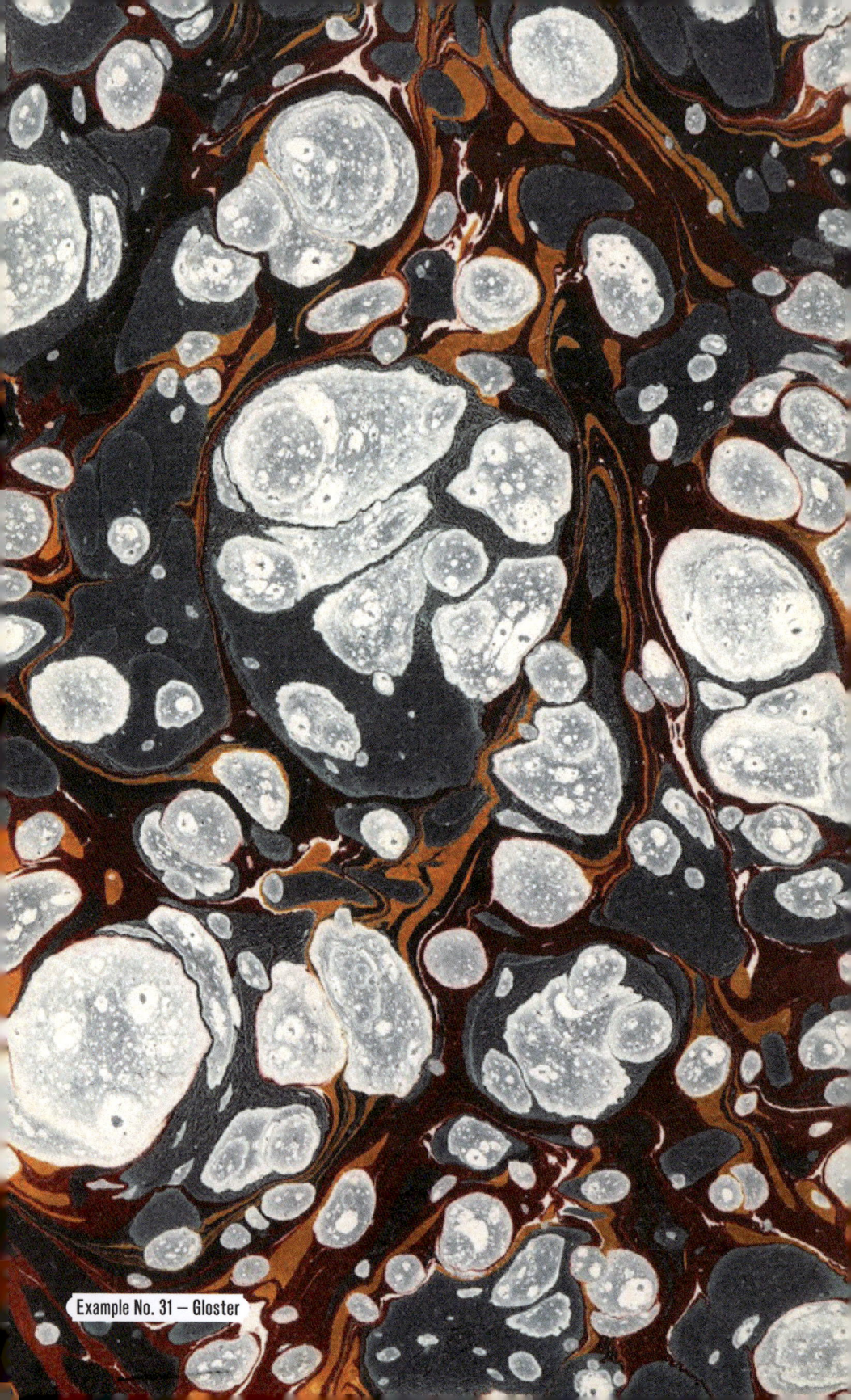

Example No. 31 — Gloster

EXAMPLE NO. 31

Gloster

This pattern is produced in precisely the same manner as the Antique Spot, with this exception, that instead of the Spot being a flat colour, i.e., a colour mixed with gall and water alone, a blue Stormont is thrown on in place of it, and no white is beaten on at the last.

Medium: gum alone.

BOOK EDGES

With regard to the preparations and manipulations of the colours, there is really no difference between book edges and paper; all the colours should, however, be ground with wax, otherwise you would find it difficult to burnish them without scratching, unless you sized them, which is objectionable for this reason, that the books would undergo being twice wetted where once would do, thereby softening the millboards and delaying the drying.

As there is no need therefore to repeat what has been already described and explained in the former part of this work, I shall limit my observations to what I consider only necessary and useful.

In the first place, it is a much easier task to marble a book edge than a perfect sheet of paper, because when you have covered the entire surface with colour, although there may be some portions faulty and imperfect, some parts may be picked out sufficiently good to permit a book edge to be taken off it, while if the whole were transferred to paper the bad or faulty parts would condemn the whole.

When plates, which are generally printed on a very soft paper, are placed at the beginning of a book or interspersed through its pages of letterpress, you must be very careful to keep the book compressed as tightly as you possibly can, and when marbled lay the book down the beginning side upwards, as the liquid has a tendency to settle round the edge of the book on the board, and if not attended to and shaken or wiped off will be apt to stain the outside leaves, as experience will prove.

For book edges you may do with a much smaller trough and also smaller quantities of colour than for paper. Should you have but few books, and those of various patterns, you had better use the solution of gum tragacanth alone to work upon, as you will be able to do any pattern upon that medium which you cannot do upon any other; besides, it will keep good longer than anything else. Your colours also for edges will look all the brighter and work the more readily by the addition of a little alcohol—gin, rum, or whisky will answer the purpose admirably, but they will be apt to evaporate or dry up more quickly. Your trough for general purposes should be about twelve inches in breadth and about twenty-four in length, the depth about two and a-half or three inches, and made according to the plan described at page 17. Supposing that you have your colours all in readiness on your solution ready for application, take the book, or books, as many as you can hold with safety, hold them tightly with the backs in your right hand and the fore-edges in your left, knock the ends on a solid block of wood, stone, or any other substance, so as to send the boards up and produce a level surface—otherwise the projection of the boards will prevent the colour from reaching the edges of the books—and let them touch the colours, the back part first, allowing the book to descend gently and gradually till it reaches the fore-edge, which you must not permit to descend below the surface at all, while the back of the book will have had a dip of about half or three-quarters of an inch, so as to produce, when gently lifted out, the appearance of a slanting wet mark on the end of the board. If you were to dip it too flat, you would most likely have a white blotch somewhere about it, caused by the imprisoned air.

In doing the fore-edge the beginner had better place the book between a pair of boards, having first thrown back the boards of the book; a pair of cutting or backing boards will answer the purpose. If you feel any diffidence, you had better tie a piece of cord round them to make all safe, but be sure to get the fore-edge as flat as possible, or you will most likely get an air-bladder in the hollow, which will greatly disfigure the appearance of your work.

If the books are not too tightly drawn in, the boards may be put back over the ledges, so as to allow them to come up flush to the fore-edge; but as some paper swells very much when wetted, it makes the ends so thick that it makes it very difficult to obtain sufficient pressure in this way on the fore-edges to keep the wet from getting into the book. However,

I leave this to your own judgment, experience alone must decide. When dipped, wipe off the superfluous moisture with a sponge; put the boards back in their places, and put them to dry, but not at the fire, as that injures the colours. Vellum or stationery work and books uncovered, or in the flat, do not, of course, require all this trouble; but still they cannot be done properly without boards, as the outside ones would be necessarily exposed to injury.

VELLUM OR STATIONERY WORK

The Large Dutch, which makes so showy an appearance on the edges of the ledgers and account books in the shop windows of the stationers, is done in a very different manner to any of the processes hitherto described.

The colours used for this description of work must be of the best quality, and must be ground with alcohol, and also mixed up with the same, combined with gall, just sufficient to make them float and spread to the required proportions. You will require no brushes, but, instead, you must provide yourself with tapering pieces of wood about the thickness of a little finger; but as this is rather a vague idea, I had better say about half an inch in thickness, tapering, but not to a point, and about four inches in length, one for each colour. Small pots will be required for these colours, capable of holding about as much as a small tea-cup. The colours required are red, orange, blue, and green. The red must be the best scarlet—drop lake, or carmine; the orange—orange lead; the blue—indigo and ultramarine; and the green—indigo and Dutch pink. These, as I before stated, should all be ground and mixed up with alcohol, adding as much gall as you find necessary to produce the required effect. The colours will be all the better for being ground a day or two before using, and kept moist. Your gum may also be a little thicker for this Large Dutch than for the other kinds of work. Having tempered your colours, and proved them by trying them on the gum, take up in your left hand the pot of colour, while, with your right, you take the stick, holding it by the thumb and two forefingers, somewhat in the way you would take up a pen, but slanting it (not, as the schoolmasters would say, over the shoulder), but quite the other way; and while you keep stirring the colour every time you dip the stick into it, taking up as much as the stick will hold, draw it steadily across the surface in sloping stripes, similar to those you would make on a smaller scale if learning to write, taking care that you do not bury the point of the stick beneath the surface;

but as you pass it over, let it just touch, so as to permit the colour to flow off as you draw it along. And instead of, as in writing, drawing the stroke commencing at the top, here you do the reverse—you commence at the bottom, and pass the stroke away from you.

The first colour you lay on should be the red. Lay on two strokes of this, almost close together; then leave a small open space; then make two more, and so on, till you have gone over as large an extent as will suffice for the book you have to marble. Next take the orange, and put on one stripe of that between each two stripes of red that are close together, filling up the intermediate spaces with alternate stripes of green and blue side by side—that is to say, there must be a green stripe and a blue stripe between each pair of red stripes. Then draw the large comb through the colours from left to right; or, if you prefer it, form a sort of feather pattern by drawing up and down a piece of wire or pointed stick at intervals of two or three inches. The following may explain more clearly the order for laying on the colours; the letters are the initials of the various colours:—

R O R G B R O R G B R O R G B R O R G B R O R.

For the Small Dutch, the colours are drawn by a tapering stick up and down through them to the shape required with a smaller comb.

Another method of doing the Large Dutch is by having a pot of white in addition to the other colours, laying them on as follows:—First, lay on stripes of red at regular distances; next, lay on orange between every alternate stripe of red; then lay on, between the stripes of red left, the green; again, right through the centre of the stripe of green make a stripe of blue; and lastly, take the pot of white and make a clean sharp stroke through the centre of the blue, draw the comb through, and you will have a very nice clean edge when washed, as all this class of work should be,—the difference between this method and the former being that, instead of laying on the green and blue side by side, the one is taken through the other, and the white through both. When well done, it looks more lively and is easier to accomplish than the other. I have seen a good deal of work of this kind done on a trough only six inches in width.

ANTIQUE (COMPLEX)

This pattern is of rather a complicated nature, and requires a little skill in its manipulation, which is very tedious; and unless the colours are in first-rate order, and your paper well adapted for the purpose, you will find the colours crack before you complete the process of laying them on the solution. The first three or four colours are sprinkled on as usual, they are then drawn with a piece of pointed stick diagonally up and down across the trough, and then crosswise again at proper distances; the green or dominant colour is then sprinkled all over, or in pods at t certain distances; then with a smaller brush the lighter colour is knocked on in small quantities at measured distances; and lastly, white is beaten on over the whole, in the same manner as for ordinary antique. Some have given it the undignified name of Kidney Pattern: it looks very well when properly made, but is little used at present.

ON THE ADAPTATION OF THIS ART FOR THE MANUFACTURE OF PAPER-HANGINGS

That this process might be adapted for the purposes of house decoration, with regard to its suitability for halls, plinths, and staircases, has been proved by experiments made some years ago, and which met with general approbation from all to whose notice the patterns were Submitted in that department of useful ornamentation, one house of business alone being of opinion that they could find a ready market for it; but unless it could be supplied to them by wagon-loads, it would be of no use to introduce it. As it was not possible at that time to do this, from the impossibility of obtaining competent hands, it fell to the ground. Whether it may at some future time be revived, it is not possible to say; but if it ever should be, there must be a wide field open in that direction for the exercise of talent, and the development of artistic skill and ingenuity, which would doubtless in time meet with its reward, especially if a few artistic touches were applied by hand, in conjunction with the natural and easy flow of the colours peculiar to this process, and which no hand work can equal or imitate, but which might be improved in effect by a judicious and skilful combination of both. Of course, the patterns, and everything connected therewith, would be on a much larger scale than has hitherto been attempted.

MARBLED CLOTH

In the year 1851, during the time of the first great Exhibition, after numerous experiments, it was found that this process might be applied to dyed and plain cloth, so extensively used in the binding of books, and on some of the coloured cloths the effects produced surpassed in brilliancy any that had hitherto been executed upon paper. When first introduced to the notice of a few of the principal bookbinders and publishers of London, it was received with the most cordial approval and orders to a large amount were promised; but these flattering indications of success ultimately contributed to its failure, and although orders to a large amount were taken and executed, those in whose hands the control and management, or rather mismanagement, was vested, thinking that from the great demand for the article they could command any terms they thought proper to exact, proceeded to impose such arbitrary terms that the trade, in general, turned against it, and a reaction took place which they were not able to hinder or check, and a patent having been taken out, not only for Great Britain but also for other countries, it resulted in a loss. The writer, who first brought it to perfection, being under an engagement with the firm for a term of years, was excluded from any participation in the benefits, and his advice was rejected, though afterwards, when too late, it was regretted it had not been followed. The patent and the firm are now both extinct.[1]

For the sides of half-bound extra work, it certainly is an improvement, both as regards durability and appearance; of course it is a little more expensive but in the binding of a good book that is an item not worthy of consideration.

---

1   Woolnough was the manager of the Patent Marbled Cloth Manufactory.

One proof of the success which attended its first introduction may be adduced from the fact that another manufacturer of bookbinders' cloth, finding that he must not infringe the patent, attempted to imitate some of the patterns by printing, but the results produced fall far behind the hand-work, and are very imperfect imitations at best, the only advantage being that pieces may be printed in any length, while those which are *bona fide* marbled are limited to a yard or two in length at most.

The following transcript is from Woolnough's lecture, "The Art of Marbling," given in 1878.

THE ART OF MARBLING[1]

By C. W. Woolnough

The subject I am about to bring before your notice this evening, viz., the art of marbling, as applied to paper for bookbinding, and for the ornamentation of book edges, is one of which, in the general sense of the term, very little is known, and very little is recorded. Its origin and antecedents are involved in obscurity, and I have sought in vain for reliable information on this point.

Having seen some marbled paper on books bearing dates of a couple of centuries or more ago, I once thought it probable that might have been the time when it was first brought into use; but, as it is very possible that these books might have been either re-bound or repaired at a more recent date, when the marbled paper was applied, I gave up that idea as one on which no reliance could be placed. I was told many years ago, by an old man, that marbled paper of the old Dutch pattern used to be imported into this country from Holland; and, in order to evade payment of the duty, which was rather heavy, sheets of it were wrapped round small packages of toys, and thus passed free; these sheets being afterwards smoothed out, pressed, and sold at a highly remunerative price to the bookbinders; and I have occasionally met with some of these ancient specimens, which retained a marvellous softness and brilliancy of colour, and displayed a considerable amount of skill in their manipulation.

---

1   *Journal of the Society of Arts*, January 25, 1878.

To anyone seeing the process for the first time, it appears to be very easy, indeed I have heard many people observe, "Oh, any fool could do that, if they did but know how to mix up the colours." I am quite willing to admit this, but to mix the colours, and to keep them in good working order, is not quite so easy after all, as the chemical changes which are constantly taking place, and the influences of the atmosphere, will speedily prove.

I will now endeavour to tell you what the process is.

Marbling is the art of producing certain patterns or figures, by the means of colours so prepared as to float upon a surface of mucilage. Although several colours may be thrown, sprinkled, or laid on together, or one after another, yet they will still each retain a distinct position, and will not mix either with each other or with the vehicle on which they float; and thus, while floating, they may be formed into the desired pattern before being transferred to the paper, which is accomplished by gently and carefully laying the sheet of paper down gradually upon the floating colours, which will instantly adhere to the paper; and, when lifted out on a rod or lath, will leave the surface of the mucilage free for a repetition of the process.

Now we must observe that this is a very different thing to the manufacture of room or wallpapers, which is usually designated by the name of paper staining; this is all done with blocks of wood, cut and carved out by hand, and is, in fact, a kind of printing, so that an exact repetition of the same device can be produced *ad libitum;* whereas, in this process, the effects being natural, no two can be found exactly alike, though called by the same name, and passing for the same pattern; nor could any artist, with all his skill, produce a facsimile of what may be accomplished by this method in a few minutes, were he to try for a whole month, or longer. Now, there are two questions which we will take into our consideration this evening, and the first is, "What is it that causes the colour to float and spread out upon the surface of the mucilage?" and, secondly, "What is it that prevents the colours from commingling or running into each other when they fall one upon another?" What is it that keeps each colour clear and distinct, though several may be thrown on at the same time, and though they may be even twisted round with a piece of wire, or pointed stick, as I shall show you presently. There are mysteries in all the operations of nature, some of which are very beautiful, and interesting to an inquiring mind. The great Michael Faraday himself, in one of his letters to me, observes, in reference to this art, "I feel much interest in the subject, not only on account of its associations with my early occupation of bookbinding, but also on account of the beautiful principles of natural philosophy which it involves;" so, however it may be despised, if it was not despised by, but was an object of interest to, that great and good man, surely it cannot be beneath our notice either. I will now endeavour, in a plain and simple way, to explain to you the so-called mysteries of this process, which some have so long and so jealously concealed from the vulgar gaze, and I verily believe that its extreme simplicity was the principal cause of the extreme watchfulness maintained by those who then practised it. Fifty years ago, it was almost as difficult to get a sight of the inside of a marbling establishment as it would be to get into the presence of Royalty; every crack and aperture, nay even the very keyholes, were stopped up or obscured, to prevent any glimpse being obtained as to the method by which it was accomplished; and, as comparatively few were in possession of its secrets, it was a very remunerative craft, and good profits were realised.

When I was about 13 years of age, I accompanied an individual who was going to fetch some books which had been sent out to be marbled; when we arrived they were not all finished, and your humble servant was admitted into the sanctum to wait for the remainder. I was so stricken with wonder and admiration at the sight, that I resolved in my own mind not to rest till I had found out how to do it. I will not now take up time by telling you of all the failures and the disappointments I met with; but at length, by unremitting toil and persevering efforts, I was in the end rewarded with success, and though for long time the results were very imperfect, yet I could perceive that I had got hold of the root of the matter, and, after much practice, I, of course, approached nearer a perfect result; and as I was indebted to no one for the knowledge I had obtained, in the year 1853 I published a small work on the subject, which gave great offence to the fraternity, on account of its truthfulness, and the way in which the various kinds of marbling were set forth, and the manner of their accomplishment explained. You see here now before me a shallow vessel or trough, about 2 ½ or 3 inches in depth; it contains a thin mucilage. Now, there are several kinds of mucilage, viz., first, and most important, gum tragacanth, called by some gum dragon; secondly, linseed or flax seed; thirdly, Irish or Carrageen moss; fourthly, a seed, called among the initiated, flea seed, the name being given on account of its great resemblance to that well-known but troublesome insect, but really the seed of a kind of plantago, cultivated, I believe, in the south of France, and much superior to linseed, on the ground that it retains its properties a much longer time; besides one tablespoonful will produce as much mucilage as half-a-pint of the linseed. The mucilage used this evening is a solution of gum tragacanth. It requires two or three days to dissolve, and requires to be frequently stirred or beaten up during that time, in order to break the lumps and to combine the gum with the water, after which it must be strained through a fine hair or muslin sieve before using.

I shall now proceed to show you by what means the colour is made to float and expand upon the surface of this liquid, but first will prove that, without some other agency than water in the mixing of the colours they will neither float nor spread, and there is but one thing at present known that will affect this. It is a very simple though subtle and powerful fluid—no expensive or elaborately prepared article; it is purely a production of nature, being nothing more or less than the gall of an animal. Ox-gall is the sort generally used; it is the easiest to be obtained and is within the reach of all who may wish to try the experiment. I will not say that the gall of a horse may not be as effective as that of an ox, having never tried it; but I have tried the gall of sheep, and proved it much weaker, so that ox-galls diluted with water would be quite as good as that; but there is sometimes a great difference in the galls taken from different animals, some being far more powerful in their operation than others. The gall of one animal may be thick and ropy, which is objectionable, while that from another may be beautifully fluid, which is more pleasant to use. When fresh, it has no unpleasant odour, but when stale it is anything but agreeable, though none the worse for the required purpose; indeed, I consider it preferable.

I will now proceed to show you the action of the gall. I first draw this thin flat piece of wood, called a skimmer, over the surface of the solution trough. You ask me why I do this? I reply because while I have been reading or speaking there has been forming on the top of the liquid a film or thin skin which, though imperceptible to the eye, is quite sufficient to frustrate the proper result. I now take a colour mixed only with water and allow a few drops to fall; It neither floats nor spreads, but falls to the bottom of the trough. I now pour a little gall into the same colour and again sprinkle some on the surface, this time, however, it floats and spreads all over the surface of the mucilage. I just lay on that a piece of white paper, and pouring into a glass a little water, I add a few drops of gall, and with a brush sprinkle it over the portion of the surface of colour not covered by the paper, and you will see that it has divided the colour into veins, thereby showing the effect produced by the gall when it is mixed with the colours; and in order to enable you to see the effect of this more vividly, I will lay on another piece of paper by the side of the first, and lifting the two out simultaneously, the operation or effect of the gall is clearly made manifest. This is the foundation of the whole process; this is the root from which all the branches spring, and although there may be other ingredients required to produce various effects, still these two simple productions of Nature—the gum and the gall— constitute the life and soul of this (as the late Dr. Normandy designated it) "pretty mysterious art."

In order to exemplify this more fully, permit me to give you another illustration, which I think will satisfy you as to the correctness of my statements. Take five different colours, viz., red, black, orange, blue, and buff. The first colour, red, is mixed with a small proportion of gall in it; the second with a little more; the third, orange, with more still; and so on, each succeeding colour requiring additional proportions of this fluid, in order to enable it to find a place for itself by displacing, or pushing aside, the previous colours, and driving them up into a smaller compass, thereby rendering them more intense and solid, and better adapted for their formation into such devices as the operator may desire.

First, I will apply the red; it spreads out over almost the whole surface of the solution, so that you can hardly perceive it, but I will, nevertheless, just lay down a small piece of paper after each colour, that you may see the effect more definitively when transferred to the paper than you can possibly do as it floats on the trough. Next comes the black. Thirdly, the orange; this is very plainly seen as it falls. Fourthly, the blue. And lastly, the buff, these comprise all the colours required for the production of some well-known kinds of papers, but still the pattern is not complete, and I shall have to repeat the process I have just gone through, and continue the manipulations from the point at which we left off, till something like a definite result is obtained. As I observed before, Dame Nature is a very fantastic creature to have to deal with, and the farther we go into the subject, the stronger will be the proofs of this statement.

Now, after laying on all the colours, it rests entirely with the operator what shall be produced after all, for out of these few colours, as they now lie floating on the surface, a diversity of results can be obtained quite distinct the one from the other, and with a piece of pointed stick, a comb, or a piece of wire, you may indulge your fancy to almost any extent; and then, by diversifying the colours or the arrangement of the colours, an almost infinite variety of combinations and changes may be produced. Having disposed of the first question, viz., what is it that causes the colour to float and spread out upon the surface of the solution P we come to the second. What is it that keeps the colours from commingling, when they fall one upon the other ? or in other words, what is it that keeps each colour clear and distinct, though several may even be thrown on at the same time, and though they may be even twisted round, nay, almost stirred with a pointed stick, every colour retaining its perfect individuality, though in so very minute a degree as to require a magnifying glass to reveal it. My humble opinion is this. The moment the colour touches the surface of the mucilage, it displaces a portion of mucilage itself, which forms a kind of bulwark or barrier around it, and thus prevents it meeting with the colours which had been previously put on, so that, were you to put on a yellow and immediately follow with a blue, there would be no signs of a green being produced, although if you were to mix the two colours together before you put them on to the mucilage you would have a decided green at once.

I have no intention of entering into a discussion upon acids and alkalies, chemical affinities, and combinations, as I do not profess to understand them, except in their action upon the materials connected with my present subject, and I think it better, therefore, to confess my ignorance at once on this point, than to occupy your time by pretending to explain anything beyond my power. This I know, that the more potent acids, such as sulphuric, nitric, muriatic, &c., would disarrange, nay, destroy, every attempt to produce the results I have just now exhibited, or may attempt to produce this evening. I believe acids are used in some of the cheap papers imported into this country from the Continent, but they find but little favour among competent judges of the art. A little alkali, however, is sometimes useful to correct the acidity in some of the colours, when they have not been sufficiently washed in the making, as also to soften the hardness of the water used in the preparation of the mucilage; but I will pass on to another peculiar feature in this process, and that is the very remarkable effect produced by a slight motion of the hand of the operator, while he is in the act of laying the paper down upon the colour as it floats, without the aid of any instrument whatever. This class of marbling has been discovered and introduced but little more than half a century, and was, in reality, quite a new feature in the art. It succeeded amazingly, obtained high prices, and an almost unprecedented demand, which continued for several years, until, as more people got into the way of doing it, and more expeditious movements were attained, it came into such general use that the public got tired of it, and it is now seldom used, except on work of a lower standard. The name given to it was Spanish; we are not to suppose by this that the name has any reference to its nationality, but simply to distinguish it from other kinds then in use, as French, Italian, Dutch, &c. Various stories are told concerning the way by which it was first discovered, some of them being ridiculous enough. I will just allude to two of them. The first is as follows:—One man was intently engaged on his work, and had all his colours laid on; just as he was on the point of laying down the sheet of paper, some other drove violently against him or the trough, by which the whole surface was agitated and set in motion like the waves of the sea, producing an effect which excited further inquiry and study, resulting in the production of this very pretty description of marbling. I have also been informed that the first that was made was produced in the following manner. "When all was prepared for the laying on of the papers, one man got under the trough and shook it, so as to produce a wavy motion, when the paper was instantly applied by another, producing the wave-like appearance; these were, however, so broad and irregular, when compared with what is done by the present method, besides occupying two to do the work of one, that it fell into disuse as soon as the improved method was brought to light. Another story is this, and I am sorry to say that there is a considerable probability of there being some truth in it, as that bane of society, strong drink, is indulged to excess by many of those who are engaged in this calling. One of these unfortunates, with trembling hand and shattered nerves, went to his employment one morning, after a bout of drinking, driven, I suppose, by necessity; and when he came to lay the paper down, his palsied hand shook so much that he spoiled, as he admitted, every sheet of paper he attempted to make. Some of these attracted the attention of the principal, to whom the cause was explained, and the light thrown on the subject gave rise to further investigation, till at last the perfect development was obtained. I do not vouch for the truth of these narratives. I give them to you just as I received them, and hold myself in no way responsible for their veracity, but leave you to form your own opinion, and judge for yourselves. But I must pass over some very interesting varieties, as I would not trespass beyond the usual bounds. I should like, however, to show you the way in which this Spanish is varied, which I think will interest you when you see how trifling a thing makes a great difference. In this experiment, I will produce on one piece of paper the lights and shadows in diagonal lines, while on the other they will be shaded something like watered silk.

There is one more variety to illustrate, of quite a different character to any of the former; in this several colours are put on at once without the aid of brushes, and by this method, a considerable degree of uniformity can be obtained. It is one of the oldest styles of work revived and modernised and is in great demand at the present time for antique and the better class of binding. It is called old Dutch and consists of several varieties, some large, some small, some curled, some not, but all, so far as the laying on of the colours is concerned, conducted on the same principle, the varieties being produced by the manipulations after the colours have been laid on.

Now, if you will attentively observe a whole sheet of this class, you will perceive that the colours are not scattered promiscuously over the whole, but follow each other in a kind of regular succession, in a diagonal direction across the sheet, red being the preponderating colour. In order to accomplish this, a number of little pots, or tins, are required, about 1½ or 2 inches wide, and 2 or 3 inches deep. Small jam pots will do very well. You will also require two frames, fitted with wooden pegs, and placed at regular distances apart—about four or more inches—having the appearance of a farmer's harrow in miniature. The frames of pegs must correspond with each other in every respect, so that, if you made an impression with one frame on a sheet of paper, the other ought to fit exactly upon the impressions produced by the first; because the colours you will have to apply with the second frame will be placed exactly in the centre of the colour put on with the first.

The pots must now be arranged in two divisions, an equal number in each, and adjusted so as the teeth or pegs of the frames will drop in the centre of each pot, as you will have to give a motion to the frame to stir the colours, as they soon settle; one of these divisions of pots must be half filled with white or ground pipeclay, the other with three different colours, arranged in the following order, the number varying according to the size of your paper. Y stands for yellow, B blue, G green:—

G	Y	G	Y	G	Y
Y	B	Y	B	Y	B
G	Y	G	Y	G	Y
Y	B	Y	B	Y	B
G	Y	G	Y	G	Y

Instead of having pots for the white, you may have a trough or vessel the size of your frame, about three inches deep, for the reception of that colour, which will answer the purpose equally well and with less trouble.

The red, which is the first colour to be applied, must be sprinkled on with a brush, and the surface well covered, then lift carefully the first frame, consisting of the white, giving it a rotary motion so as to stir up the mixture, and let the extremities of the pegs with the colour on them just touch the surface of the mucilage in every part; put it back in the colour, and quickly take the other charged with the three colours, and in like manner let that touch just in the middle of the spots of white, then with a tapering piece of wood—the handle of a brush for example—draw the colours in a parallel direction up and down, from front to back, after which draw the comb through the colour, from left to right, and the pattern is complete, unless you think fit to add curls or any other device, which, of course, must be left to your own discretion.

Thus far we have gone without the aid of any other agent in the colours than gall, and there are many more varieties to be produced by the same material. There are also some very pleasing results to be obtained by the use of other agencies, but it is impossible to compress them into the compass of one single paper. I could have enlarged on this part of the subject tonight, and have mentioned many strange and interesting facts regarding this art. What I have so imperfectly revealed tonight has, I hope, proved that there are many things in everyday life which escape our notice, simply because they are common, but from which we might draw much that both interest and enlighten us, if we would but exercise the powers with which God has invested us, and placed us so far above the inferior creation. With one more experiment, I will now close this paper, and that will simply be to show that whenever the paper is wetted with the solution, no colour will adhere to it while the moisture remains on its surface. I will now wet some part of the paper, and after preparing a surface of colour on the trough, will lay on this sheet of paper, and, on lifting it out, you will see that the part wetted will be bare of colour, while the part that remained dry is perfectly marbled.

* * *

The various methods of producing the different descriptions of marble paper were illustrated by Mr. Woolnough, who made a number of specimens in the room. Examples of the printed paper were also exhibited, as well as specimens of the materials employed.

Discussion

A Member asked if the marbling of book edges was done by the same process as had been shown for the manufacture of marbled paper Mr. Woolnough said the operation was exactly the same, except that the book edge had to be put a little lower into the trough in order to ensure the whole surface being covered, otherwise there would be the probability of a bubble of air being included which would spoil the effect. The book was put down into the solution until the operator saw the fore-edge touch the surface. There was no difference in the preparation of the surface or in the manipulation. There was plenty of room for a second paper in which other materials used might be described, and if he ever he had the honour of illustrating the subject again, he would go into the matter of book edges, which he had simply omitted for want of time.

The Chairman said he was sure all present would concur in the vote of thanks which he would beg leave to propose to Mr. Woolnough for his interesting paper. It had shown him that a subject which at first sight seemed to be one of very limited interest, might, by a person well acquainted with it and who could speak lucidly upon it, be made one of considerable interest to those who heard it. It had been illustrated in a very skillful manner, and they had heard incidentally, also, that drunken men might sometimes have their uses. He hoped that anecdote would not be misapplied, but it might be a comfort to those who were in the habit of indulging to find that they were of some use occasionally. The effects produced by this process were, more or less, dependent upon chance; but it had occurred to him that if it were taken up by artistic people, they might make something more of it than had hitherto been done.

The vote of thanks having been passed unanimously, Mr. Woolnough thanked the audience for their attention and appreciation, and the proceedings terminated.

INDEX

A

account books 10, 97
   size
      gum tragacanth 12
alcohol 94, 97
alum 15, 22, 88
   size paper after marbling 16
Antique Complex pattern 99
Antique Curled pattern 59, 61
Antique pattern 59
   size
      gum tragacanth 16
Antique Spots pattern 56, 57–59, 58
Antique Straight pattern 59, 60
Antique Zigzag pattern 62–64, 63–65, 64–66
arsenic 9

B

beeswax 17
   preparration for grinding 17
blue black 4
Blue Italian 26, 27
boiled oil 14
bookbinders' cloth 22, 103–104
book edges 5, 6, 30, 93, 93–95
Brazil wood 6
British pattern 77–79
   size 16
brown 7
Brunswick green 4, 10
burnish 93
burnt Oxford ochre 3, 6, 7, 10
burnt sienna 4
burnt Turkey umber 4, 10

C

carmine 3, 4
carrageen moss 13
chalk 6
China clay white 4, 11
Chinese blue 3, 7, 9
chrome green 4, 10
chrome yellow 4, 8
Coccus cacti 5
cochineal 5
colours, grinding 16–17
colours: list of those used in marbling
   blacks 4
   blues 3
   browns 4
   greens 4
   orange 4
   reds 3
   whites 4
   yellows 4
combs 18–22, 20, 21, 43
   bottom combs 18–19, 21
   construction of 19–21
   Nonpareil comb 19
   top 18–19
common lamp black 4
crimson 5
Curl pattern 47–50, 49–52, 50
   size
      gum tragacanth 16

D

double rake 63
Drag Spanish pattern 41–42
drop ivory black 4, 9
drop lake 3, 5, 6
Dutch paper 2

Dutch pattern 5
  large 97–98
  size
    gum tragacanth 12, 16
  small 98
Dutch pink 4, 8, 9

E

emerald green 4, 9
English pink 4, 8
Eton College xiv
Extra Spanish pattern 41–42

F

Faraday, Michael xiii
flake white 4, 11
flax seed 12
flea seed 4, 12–13, 16, 26, 30, 33, 40, 55, 77, 87
flint 15, 22
fore-edge 94
French pattern 79–85
  oil 14
  size 16
  trough 18

G

gall water 87
glazing 15, 22
Gloster pattern 90, 91–92
glue 22
Great Exhibition 103
green lake 4, 10
gum dragon 11
gum elect 11
gum tragacanth 11, 12, 15, 16, 26, 30, 40, 43, 47, 55, 57, 77, 87, 93
  preparation 12
  preserve 15
  thicken with alum 15

H

half-bound 103
Hinks, Thomas 6
Holland 2

I

indigo 3, 7, 8, 9, 10
Irish Moss 13
Italian Four Veins pattern 24, 29–31
Italian pattern
  size 16
  trough 18

K

kerosine 15
Kidney Pattern. *See* Antique Complex pattern

L

lamp black 9
lead 10
ledgers 97. *See also* account books
linseed mucilage. *See* flax seed
linseed oil 14
lokao (Chinese green) 8

M

mercury 5

N

Nonpareil pattern 43, 43–46, 48
  comb 19
  size
    Gum Tragacanth 12, 16
  trough 18

O

Old Dutch pattern 8, 65–76
olive oil 14
orange chrome 4
orange lead 4, 6, 10
Oxford ochre 7, 8
ox gall 13, 13–14, 14–15, 25, 29, 30, 33, 34, 91

P

paper
  Glazing 22
  half-sized 22
  hard-sized 22

paper-hangings
    Manufacture of 101
paraffin 15
Paris white 4, 11
Patent Marbled Cloth Manufactory ix, 103
peach wood lake 3, 6
Pepper, J. H. ix, xiii
pipe clay 4, 11
plantago. *See* flea seed
prussian blue 3, 8
purple 5, 7

Q
quercitron bark 8

R
rake
    peg-rake 43
raw oxford ochre 4, 8, 9
rock oil 15
rose pink 3, 6
Royal Cornwall Gazette, the xi
Royal Polytechnic Institution ix, xiv
Royal Society at Connaught House xiv
Royal Society of Arts, Journal of the x
    lecture 105–115

S
scarlet 5
Scientific American x
Shell pattern 63, 79–85
    blue Shell, small 79, 80
    oil 14
    size 16
sizing paper after marbling 22, 93
skimmer 18
soap
    pale 22
    white curd (castile) 17
Spanish 32, 33, 38, 39–40, 40, 86
Spanish, Lace pattern 36, 37
Spanish pattern 32–35, 33–36, 38–40, 39–41
    size 16
    trough 18
Spanish pattern, fancy 36–37, 37

Spanish with Shell pattern 86
Spanish with Shell veins 81
stationery 5, 95, 97–99
stone ochre 7
Stormont pattern 87–88, 89–91
    Blue Stormont 87

T
Thorpe, Edward, Sir 3, 5, 8, 9, 10
troughs 17–18
turpentine, Spirits of 15, 87, 88

U
ultramarine 3, 7

V
vegetable lamp black 4, 9
vellum 95, 97–99
vermilion 3, 5

W
water
    hard water 16
    rain water 16
West End pattern 54–56
    size 16
white 11
whiting 6, 8
workspace arrangement 21–22

Y
yellow lake 4, 8, 9

Z
Zebra pattern 51–53

*The
Whole Art of Marbling as Applied
to Paper, Book Edges, Etc.*

Written by C. W. Woolnough

Edited and annotated by
Six Penny Graphics, Fredericksburg, Virginia.

Composed in Adobe Caslon Pro
and SchoolBook.

Also Available from Six Penny Graphics

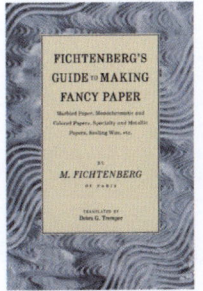

Fichtenberg's Guide to Making Fancy Paper

By M. Fichtenberg
Translated by Debra G. Tremper

6 × 9 | 242 pages | full color
ISBN: 978-1-7326595-6-8

The Progress of the Marbling Art from Technical Scientific Principles

By Josef Halfer

6 × 9 | 140 pages | full color
ISBN: 978-1-7326595-0-6

Formulas for Bookbinders

By Louis H. Kinder

6 × 9 | 136 pages | black and white
ISBN: 978-1-7326595-2-0

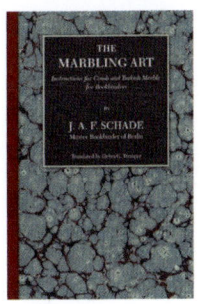

The Marbling Art: Instructions for Comb and Turkish Marble for Bookbinders

By J. A. F. Schade

5 × 8 | 42 pages | full color
ISBN: 978-1-7326595-3-7

Printed in Great Britain
by Amazon